Lively Bible Lessons
for Preschoolers

Edited by Cindy S. Hansen

Group *Books*

Loveland, Colorado

Lively Bible Lessons for Preschoolers
Copyright © 1991 by Group Publishing, Inc.

Credits
Edited by Cindy S. Hansen
Cover and interior designed by Jill Christopher
Illustrations by Jan Knudson

Unless otherwise noted, Scriptures quoted from **The Everyday Bible, New Century Version**, copyright © 1987, 1988 by Word Publishing, Dallas, Texas 75039. Used by permission.

Library of Congress Cataloging-in-Publication Data
Lively Bible lessons for preschoolers / edited by Cindy S. Hansen.
   p.   cm.
  ISBN 1-55945-067-3
  1. Bible—Study. 2. Children—Religious life. 3. Children—Conduct of life.
 I. Hansen, Cindy S. II. Group Books (Firm)
BS600.2.L533 1991
268'.432—dc20

91-21658
CIP
AC

15 14 13 12 11 10 9   04 03 02 01 00

Printed in the United States of America.

Visit our Web site: www.grouppublishing.com

CONTENTS

Part 3: A Lively Look at My Faith

Part 4: A Lively Look at Celebrations

INTRODUCTION

Welcome to a resource filled with lively, active Bible lessons for preschool children ages 3 to 5. Here are fun sessions that'll hold your kids' attention and teach self-esteem-building, friendship-boosting, faith-developing topics.

Lively Bible Lessons for Preschoolers offers Sunday school teachers, vacation Bible school teachers and any leader of young children, 20 simple-to-follow lessons that combine lively learning, colorful art projects and scrumptious snacks.

This book is divided into these four parts:

● **Part 1: A Lively Look at Myself**—Preschoolers are growing and facing new experiences daily. This section covers topics that help young children with fear, responsibility, envy and self-esteem.

● **Part 2: A Lively Look at My Relationships**—This section helps preschoolers look past themselves to others. Topics include kindness, helping those who are hurting, sharing, friendship, feelings and caring for God's world.

● **Part 3: A Lively Look at My Faith**—Preschool children are interested in God, the church and their developing faith. Faith-building topics include heaven, prayer, God's love, forgiveness, and more about God and his son, Jesus.

● **Part 4: A Lively Look at Celebrations**—People of all ages love to celebrate special occasions. This section offers Bible lessons and celebrations for birthdays, Easter, Thanksgiving and Christmas.

THE LIVELY BIBLE LESSONS

The lessons in *Lively Bible Lessons for Preschoolers* each contain eight to 10 fast-paced activities for young children with short attention spans. No activity lasts longer than six minutes. The lessons include the following elements:

● **Introduction**—One to two paragraphs that introduce the lesson's topic.

● **A Powerful Purpose**—A short statement of the lesson's objective. The purpose tells you what your children will learn.

● **A Look at the Lesson**—An outline including activity titles and estimated completion time. These times may vary depending on your group's size.

● **A Sprinkling of Supplies**—A list of all items you'll need for the lesson. You'll probably want to keep a few general supplies in your room: crayons, paper, paints, newspapers, old shirts for paint aprons, pencils and tape.

● **The Lively Lesson**—Quick, active, reflective, scripture-based activities. Lessons start with an opening experience to set the mood for the lesson. Kids experience the topics through active learning, using their senses of hearing, seeing, smelling, tasting and feeling.

Lessons include participation Bible stories, action-packed memory verses, action songs to familiar tunes, art projects and snacks.

● **Handouts**—All necessary handouts are included. They're easy to use and you have permission to photocopy them for local church use.

Enjoy *Lively Bible Lessons for Preschoolers*. Use and adapt the Bible lessons for any gathering of preschool children. Watch kids develop self-esteem, meet new friends and grow in their faith. Have fun teaching topics in an active, lively and meaningful way!

PART 1:
A LIVELY LOOK
at MYSELF

WHAT CAN I DO?

Even small children like to feel as if they have jobs all their own, or as if they're in charge. Take advantage of children's desire to be in charge and introduce them—in an enjoyable way—to doing good things. Help them see how they can honor God by doing what pleases him.

A POWERFUL PURPOSE

Preschool children will understand why it's important to do our part for God.

A LOOK AT THE LESSON

1. Our Band (up to 6 minutes)
2. Do Your Part (up to 5 minutes)
3. Partner Pals (up to 6 minutes)
4. Being Faithful (up to 5 minutes)
5. Team Tug (up to 6 minutes)
6. Helping Each Other (up to 5 minutes)
7. Our Part (up to 6 minutes)
8. Responsible Snacks (up to 6 minutes)

A SPRINKLING OF SUPPLIES

Gather a Bible, bed sheet, ribbon, several colors of yarn, crayons, glue, hole punch, photocopies of the handout, plastic sandwich bags, peanuts, raisins, M&M's, pretzels, a large bowl, napkins, juice and cups. You'll also need enough metal spoons and pan lids for your whole class.

THE LIVELY LESSON

1. Our Band

(You'll need two metal spoons each for half of the children and two pan lids each for the other half.)

Greet children as they enter. Give each child either two spoons or two pan lids.

Once everyone has an "instrument," organize your band. All spoons sit together; all lids sit together. Point to the spoons and let them play their best! Motion them to stop, then point to the lids and have them play their best. Motion them to stop.

Tell band members you also want them to sing. Have them put their instruments down on the floor, then practice singing "Hallelu, Hallelu." Assign one half the "Hallelu" part and the other half the "Praise ye the Lord" part. Practice singing the song "Hallelu, Hallelu." If you don't know this song, teach kids another praise chorus you know.

After kids know the song, add instruments and make a joyful noise to the Lord.

2. Do Your Part

Gather the instruments, then have kids sit in a circle. Say: **Everyone who sang the "Hallelu" part in the song, raise your hand.** (Pause) **Now everyone who sang the "Praise ye the Lord" part, raise your hand.** (Pause) **What would have happened** if we reached the "Praise ye the Lord" part and no one sang? Would the song be as much fun? Let's try it and see.

Sing the song one time through without the "Praise ye the Lord" part.

Say: **That wasn't as much fun as before, was it? It was kind of confusing too. We weren't sure when we were supposed to sing. We needed everyone to do his or her part, to be responsible. Doing what we say we'll do is important. It's like keeping a promise. What happens when you don't keep a promise?**

Listen to answers such as people get angry, we hurt people.

3. Partner Pals

Form pairs by having everyone grab the hand of someone sitting close by. Have one child in each pair close his or her eyes. Have the other child lead his or her partner around the room, making sure the child doesn't run into anything or any other person. Stress that their job is to take care of their partners.

After about a minute, have partners switch. Allow about another minute for them to walk around the room together.

4. Being Faithful

(You'll need a Bible.)

Say: **Good job taking care of your partners! You did your jobs well.**

Gather in a circle again. Ask:

● **What could have happened if you hadn't led your partner carefully?**

● **Why is it important to be responsible, to do what you're supposed to?**

Say: **You did great! Your partners**

didn't run into anything; they were safe. You cared for your partners. You did your part. That's what God wants us to do.

Read Proverbs 21:3a: **"Do what is right and fair."**

Say: **God is pleased when we do what's right.**

Form three groups. Have one group say "do what." Have another group say "is right." Have the third group say "and fair." Repeat until children memorize the verse. Direct the kids, having them say it softly, then gradually louder.

5. Team Tug

(You'll need a bed sheet.)

If the weather is nice, play this game outside on a grassy area. If not, play on soft carpet. Inside, ask kids to remove their shoes and play in their socks.

Form two teams. Twist the sheet so it's in the shape of a rope and play tug-of-war. Do at least two or three rounds.

6. Helping Each Other

Ask: **Why was it hard pulling on the sheet?**

Say: **Just like it was hard to pull against another team, it's also hard to do what's right sometimes. Suppose your mom tells you to clean your room, but your friends ask you to play? Or, what if you're supposed to help set the table for dinner, but you wanted to watch TV? It's not always easy to do what we're supposed to do. How can we help each other do our part?**

Listen to answers such as pray for each other, help each other, share, don't ask someone to play if you know he's supposed to be helping his mom. Tell kids to go around the circle, and one at a time call each child by name to say, "Help each other."

7. Our Part

(You'll need crayons, ribbon, different colors of yarn, glue, and photocopies of the "Our Part" handout. Cut out the face on the handout and use a hole punch to punch a hole in top.)

Give one handout and crayons to each child. Read the words on it: **"Do what is right and fair."** Let children draw their own faces in the circle, then glue yarn on for hair. Help kids thread ribbon through the hole so that they can hang them up at home to remind themselves that it's important to do what's right.

8. Responsible Snacks

(You'll need a separate plastic sandwich bag filled with one of these items for each of your kids: peanuts, M&M's, raisins, pretzels. You'll also need a large bowl, napkins, juice and cups.)

Give each person a plastic bag filled with an item to make trail mix. Say: **Each one of us has an ingredient for our snack. It's your part to put your ingredient in this big bowl.**

Ask one person to put his or her ingredient in the bowl. Say: **If no one did his or her part to add to the snack, would it be as good? We each need to do our job.**

Mix the goodies and serve the trail mix on napkins. Give everyone juice to drink. Close the lesson by praying: **God, help us to do our part. Help us do what's right. Remind us to help our friends do their part too. We love you. Amen.**

by Karen M. Ball

OUR PART

"Do what is right and fair."
(Proverbs 21:3a)

GREEN WITH ENVY

Envy is a common feeling for all people, all ages. Many adults closely watch for the newest and neatest gadgets and technology, as well as the new items their neighbors buy. Little children play with their toys but want their friends' toys.

Use this lesson to help young children deal with envy. Teach preschoolers to give thanks for what they have.

A POWERFUL PURPOSE

Preschool children will learn to be happy with the things they have, not envious of other people's things.

A LOOK AT THE LESSON

1. Look at My Snack
   (up to 4 minutes)
2. See How I Feel (up to 4 minutes)
3. Envious Faces (up to 4 minutes)
4. Flannel Board Photos
   (up to 5 minutes)
5. Good for You (up to 6 minutes)
6. My Blessings (up to 6 minutes)
7. Love Is Not Envious
   (up to 5 minutes)
8. A Taste of Envy (up to 6 minutes)

A SPRINKLING OF SUPPLIES

Gather a Bible, brownies, small crackers, paper, a marker, a flannel board, pictures of Joseph and his special coat, crayons, lime Jell-O, table knives and napkins.

THE LIVELY LESSON

1. Look at My Snack

(You'll need brownies and small crackers.)

When kids arrive, gather them in a circle and pass out snacks. Half of the class receives a brownie, the other half receives a cracker. Say: **A brownie for you, a cracker for you** as you pass them out.

You'll likely hear protests from the cracker receivers, but just bear with them.

2. See How I Feel

(You'll need brownies and small crackers. Use a marker to draw a huge smile on a piece of paper. Draw a huge frown on another piece of paper.)

Hold up the smile and ask: **How many of you felt like this when I gave you a snack? Why?** Let kids respond with "I love brownies." Or, "They taste great."

Hold up the frown and ask: **How many of you felt like this? Why?** Let them respond with "I like brownies better than crackers." Or, "The brownie was bigger. I was hungry."

Give crackers to the children who already received brownies and brownies to the children who already received crackers. Say: **Remember, all good things come from God.**

Tell children that there's a word to describe our feelings when we want something someone else has. It's called envy. We feel envy when we want others' things instead of thinking of our own good gifts.

3. Envious Faces

Let everyone practice smiling and frowning. Then say: **I'm going to read some situations. If one makes you happy, show me a big smile. If one makes you feel sad, angry or full of envy, show me a big frown.**

Read these situations:

● **Your sister just got a brand-new tricycle, and you didn't get anything.**

● **A friend is eating a juicy red apple; he gives you one too.**

● **Your baby brother is surrounded by aunts and uncles who are oohing and aahing. Nobody notices you.**

● **A next-door neighbor is playing with a brand-new red truck in his brand-new sandbox. He doesn't ask you to play.**

● **You're holding your favorite book. You offer to show it to your friend.**

● **Your teacher tells you you're going to hear a good Bible story.**

4. Flannel Board Photos

(You'll need a flannel board and pictures from the story about Joseph and his special coat. Use flannel board pictures from Sunday school resources or pictures from a children's Bible or storybook. Make your own flannel board by covering a sturdy piece of cardboard—any size you want—with light-color flannel. Glue a small piece of flannel to the back of each picture you'll use.)

Before you start the story, give kids a stretcher break with the following chant. Have kids follow you in doing the actions.

Smile, (Stand and smile.)

Frown, (Bend your knees and frown.)

Smile, (Stand and smile.)

Frown, (Bend your knees and frown.)

Now it's time to sit back down. (Sit down by the flannel board.)

Tell the story of Joseph, his special coat and his envious brothers by reading Genesis 37:3-4, 14, 18-28. Use the flannel board pictures to illustrate the story.

5. Good for You

Say: **Those brothers felt a lot of envy because Joseph's dad liked him best. Joseph got a bright-colored coat and his brothers didn't. Sometimes we feel envy just like Joseph's brothers when we don't get what we want.**

Give kids a chance to say things that make them envious. For example, when a friend gets a new toy and they don't. Then tell them they're going to change envy into a good feeling. Tell kids you'll stand up and say some sort of good news, then sit down. After each bit of good news, kids are to stand up and say "I'm glad for you," then sit back down. Say:

● **Look! My dad just gave me a brand-new skateboard.**

● **My grandma is coming to take me to the zoo!**

● **My mom lets me stay up late on Friday nights.**

Add some of the situations kids previously said made them envious. After each item you say, encourage kids to say "I'm glad for you!"

Say: **Sometimes it isn't easy to be**

glad for others when they get something we'd like, but that's what God wants us to do.

6. My Blessings

(For each child, you'll need a piece of paper and crayons.)

Pass out paper to the children. Tell them each to draw a picture of a blessing—a favorite toy, pet, or somewhere nice they've been on vacation. When they finish, let them share their pictures with the others.

After each child shares, have everyone else stand up and say "I'm glad for you."

Emphasize that God blesses all of us with gifts. None of us should envy others.

7. Love Is Not Envious

Have kids learn this memory verse from 1 Corinthians 13:4: "Love is kind and does not envy." Have kids repeat the verse with you using the motions. Work with them until they can say it by themselves with you just leading the motions.

Love (Hug yourself.)

Is kind (Draw a smile on your face with both pointer fingers.)

And is not (Shake your head "no.")

Envious (Make a frown on your face.)

8. A Taste of Envy

(You'll need a shallow pan of lime Jell-O, table knives and napkins. Prepare the Jell-O according to the "Jigglers" recipe on the package.)

Help children each cut a large crescent shape out of the Jell-O. Have them each hold their crescent shape like a frown as you say: **God doesn't want us to be envious. It makes God sad when we envy others.**

Then have kids each hold their crescent shape like a smile. Say: **God wants us to be happy when others are happy. It makes God happy when we don't envy others. Let's gobble up any envy we may have.**

Encourage kids to gobble up their crescents.

Serve kids any leftovers.

Close with a prayer: **Thank you, God, for all our blessings. Take envy away and make us happy for others. Amen.**

by Ray and Cindy Peppers

FRIGHTENING FEARS

A child's world can be full of frightening things. Children don't think there's a huge, hairy, sharp-toothed monster under their bed; they know it!

Use this lesson to put fears in a new light. Let young children see they can get rid of their fears and give them to God. Help children see that God is bigger than their fears.

A POWERFUL PURPOSE

Preschool children will recognize they don't have to be afraid because God protects them.

A LOOK AT THE LESSON

1. Don't Be Afraid (up to 6 minutes)
2. Fears Drag You Down
   (up to 6 minutes)
3. Fear List (up to 4 minutes)
4. Fear Bombardment
   (up to 4 minutes)
5. Fear Protection (up to 4 minutes)
6. Get Rid of Those Fears
   (up to 4 minutes)
7. I'm Not Alone (up to 5 minutes)
8. God's Protective Love
   (up to 6 minutes)
9. Thanks for God's Love
   (up to 6 minutes)

A SPRINKLING OF SUPPLIES

Gather a Bible, blindfold, paper, marker, doll, large box, trash can, candy hearts, other snacks, crayons, ribbon, stickers, photocopies of the handout, a small box for each child, and a trash bag filled with heavy books.

THE LIVELY LESSON

1. Don't Be Afraid

(You'll need one blindfold.)

Welcome children and tell them you're going to play a game called Don't Be Afraid.

Blindfold one child. Have the other children walk in a circle around the blindfolded child. Tell the blindfolded child to try to walk out of the circle without running into anyone. When the child is about to run into someone, yell, "Stop, kids. Don't be afraid." Then have the other children squeeze together and hug the blindfolded child. Remove the blindfold and give it to another child to continue the game.

Say: **God tells us the same thing when we're afraid: "Stop, kids. Don't be afraid. I'm here to help you."**

2. Fears Drag You Down

(You'll need a trash bag filled with heavy books—heavy enough so kids have some difficulty dragging it, but not so heavy that it causes muscle strain.)

Tell children they're going to run a short relay race that'll show them how their fears can keep them from doing their best.

Form two teams. Help teams line up

at one end of the room. Give one team the heavy bag of books. Tell that team that—one person at a time—team members have to drag the bag across the room and back. The other team's members can run freely. One at a time, team members each run across the room and back, and then tag the next person on their team who repeats the process. Continue until everyone has run. First team done wins.

After the first race, give the bag of books to the other team and race again.

Afterward ask: **Which was harder—running by yourself or dragging the bag? How did you feel dragging the bag?**

Say: **Fear is like that heavy, old bag. It keeps us from doing our best, even from doing things we really want to do. Fear can keep us from doing things God wants us to do.**

3. Fear List

(You'll need a piece of paper for each child and a marker.)

Ask kids to name their fears. Some possibilities are the dark, monsters, getting lost, parents getting a divorce, a war.

Write one fear on each piece of paper. After you write one fear for each child, wad it and toss it to a child. Say: **(Name), grab that fear!** After each child has caught a fear, say: **Follow me to the next activities where we'll try to get rid of our fears.**

4. Fear Bombardment

(You'll need a doll, a large box and the wads of paper fears.)

Place a doll in the center of the room. Gather kids in a circle around it. Say: **Pretend that doll is a person who's afraid of all these fears. She's hit with them daily.**

Let kids throw their paper fears at the doll.

Next, place a large box over the doll. Ask kids to pick up a paper fear and get back to the circle. Tell them to throw the fears again and try to hit the doll.

Say: **Our fears are like these paper wads raining down on the doll. They come at us fast and hit us. But when the doll was covered by the box, the fears couldn't hit her. She was protected. God helps us like that box helped her. He covers us with his love and protection.**

5. Fear Protection

(You'll need a Bible.)

Ask: **Who protects us from our fears?** Answers could be God, Jesus, parents, friends.

Tell the story of David and Goliath found in 1 Samuel 17.

Say: **In the Bible, David was sometimes afraid. But he knew God would protect him. Listen to David's words.**

Read Psalm 27:1 from a children's Bible, or use this translation: **"The Lord is my light and the one who saves me. I fear no one. The Lord protects my life. I am afraid of no one."**

David knew that God was stronger than anything or anyone else. All we need to do is ask God to cover us—to protect us. Then the fears can't get to us. With God's help and protection, we don't need to be afraid.

6. Get Rid of Those Fears

(You'll need the wadded paper fears and a trash can.)

Gather the paper wads of fear, unwad them and read them aloud. After each fear you read, have kids stand and say: "I'm not afraid. God protects me."

Throw the fears in a trash can and say: **God gets rid of our fears.**

7. I'm Not Alone

Gather kids in a circle and stand in the middle. Say: **Our family and friends also help protect us from our fears. When we're afraid, we can tell them about it. And we can ask them to pray with us. Their love can surround and protect us. It's easier to not be afraid when we remember we're not alone.**

Choose one person to come stand in the middle with you. Both of you say: **We're not alone.** Have that child choose another child to come stand in the middle with you and all three of you say: **We're not alone.** Continue until everyone is chosen and bunched together.

8. God's Protective Love

(You'll need crayons, ribbon, tape, stickers and other decorations. Each child will need a small closed-up box with candy hearts in it and a photocopy of the "God's Box of Protective Love" handout.)

Tell kids they're going to decorate their own box to remind them that God covers them with his protective love. Give them each a box and a handout. Read the words to them: **Don't be afraid, (Name). God loves you and protects you.**

Give kids the decorating supplies. Let them color and decorate their boxes any way they want. While they're decorating, give specific words of praise as you go around to each one. Tape a handout-card to each box. Write the child's name in the space provided.

9. Thanks for God's Love

Gather in a circle and have children show their completed boxes. Reread the handout and have kids repeat the message after you: **Don't be afraid. God loves you and protects you.**

Pray: **Thank you, Father, for loving us and for being our protection against things that make us afraid. Help us to trust you. Help us not to be afraid. Amen.**

Ask children to open their boxes. When kids find the candy hearts, remind them of God's protective love. Serve other snacks with the hearts. Tell kids to think about God's love every time they eat a candy heart.

by Karen M. Ball

GOD'S BOX OF PROTECTIVE LOVE

Don't be afraid, _____

God loves you and protects you.

GOD'S BOX OF PROTECTIVE LOVE

Don't be afraid, _____

God loves you and protects you.

WHAT MAKES ME SPECIAL?

Children are unique and wonderful. Jesus tells his disciples to "let the little children come to me." In fact, they're so special that Jesus said "the kingdom of heaven belongs to people who are like these children" (Matthew 19:14).

Use this lesson to celebrate how God has made each of us special and unique. Reassure children that God's love for them is unlimited.

A POWERFUL PURPOSE

Preschool children will realize that each of us is special to God and to each other.

A LOOK AT THE LESSON

1. Run Around (up to 6 minutes)
2. Let's Make a Snowflake (up to 6 minutes)
3. Beach Ball Roll (up to 5 minutes)
4. Very Good (up to 5 minutes)
5. Happy-Face Stickers (up to 4 minutes)
6. Hugging Game (up to 4 minutes)
7. God Says I'm Special (up to 6 minutes)
8. Happy-Face Snack (up to 5 minutes)

A SPRINKLING OF SUPPLIES

Gather a tape of lively music, a tape player, white paper, blunt-end scissors, a beach ball, a Bible, happy-face stickers, crayons, glue, photocopies of the handout, milk, cups, napkins, and cookies or cupcakes with frosting happy faces.

THE LIVELY LESSON

1. Run Around

(You'll need a tape of lively music and a tape player.)

Have children jog around the room as you play music. Have children freeze where they are and all call out their names at the same time when you stop the music. The last child to say his or her name goes to the side and claps his or her hands to the music.

Start the music again and keep going in this manner until there's only one child left jogging. Vary the game by changing the actions kids do to the music. Have them skip, hop, walk and tiptoe.

Say: **You all are special. You played a fun game and clapped for each other. We're going to learn more about what makes us special and wonderful creations.**

2. Let's Make a Snowflake

(For each child, fold one square piece of white paper in half from top to bottom, in half again from side to side, and in half diagonally to form a triangle. Each child will need a blunt-end scissors.)

Ask children to sit in a circle. Show them how to make snowflakes, by

SNOWFLAKES

cutting small pieces away from the outside edges. You may need to help children make their cuts. Then open to reveal the snowflake.

Say: **Each of us is special. There's no one else like us anywhere in the world. Even people who look alike, such as identical twins, are different inside. We're like snowflakes. Did you know that no two snowflakes are alike? Let's make some snowflakes and check that out.**

Give children folded paper and blunt-end scissors. Show them how to cut the snowflakes. Compare kids' snowflakes to see if any are alike. Put each child's name on his or her snowflake.

3. Beach Ball Roll

(You'll need a beach ball.)

Say: **Just like the snowflakes, we're all different. We all have things that make us special. What are some things that make us special?**

Talk about things we can *do* such as singing, playing, smiling, laughing, praying or helping; things that we *are* such as children, daughters, sons, cheerful, smart or helpful; even physical characteristics such as eye color, hair color, freckles, strong or graceful.

Go around the circle and let each person say one thing that makes him

or her special.

Say: **Let's play a game. I'll roll a ball to someone. The person who catches the ball must say one thing that makes him or her special. That person rolls the ball to someone else who does the same. We'll continue until everyone has a turn.**

Be ready to help kids out if they can't think of anything.

4. Very Good

(You'll need a Bible.)

Say: **God made us the way we are. He made everything on the earth. What are some of God's creations?**

Let kids respond with things such as heaven, earth, animals, sky, water, flowers, trees and fish.

Read or tell the story of Creation from Genesis 1.

Say: **God made all of these things. After he made each one, he said it was good. And after God made people, he looked at his creation and said it was very good. God thinks we all are very special, because he made us to be like him.**

Read Genesis 1:31 from a children's Bible, or read this version: "God looked at everything he had made, and it was very good."

Ask kids to go around the room shaking each other's hands and say, "God thinks you're very good."

5. Happy-Face Stickers

(You'll need a happy-face sticker for each person.)

Say: **We need to remind each other that we're special. What are some ways we can do that?**

Help kids think of ways such as hugging, kissing, saying thank you, giving a gift, doing something nice for a person.

Divide into pairs by saying: **I'll count to three. In those three seconds you have to grab the hand of someone who's standing close by you. But you can only hold one other hand. Ready? One, two, three. Got a partner?**

Give each child a happy-face sticker. Have each child put the sticker on his or her partner's hand and say, "Smile, you're special."

6. Hugging Game

(You'll need a tape of lively music and a tape player.)

Ask children to stand in a circle, facing inward. Play the lively music. Have one child walk around the outside of the circle, gently patting each child on the back as he or she passes, until the music stops. When the music stops, have the child hug the person he or she is behind and say, "You're special." Then have those two children switch places and continue the game.

Let each person have a chance to walk around the circle.

7. God Says I'm Special

(You'll need crayons and the "God Says I'm Special" handout.)

Give each person a handout and crayons. Say: **This handout says "God Says I'm Special" across the top. There's space for you to draw your picture. The words say "Just like snowflakes are unique and one of a kind, I'm one of a kind." Genesis 1:31 is written on the bottom. Remember, God created people and said they were very good—very special.**

Let kids draw their picture. If you want, you could take kids' pictures with an instant-print camera and place them on the handout instead of having kids draw.

8. Happy-Face Snack

(For each child, you'll need a cookie or cupcake with a frosting happy face on it. You'll also need milk, cups and napkins.)

Serve the happy-face snack. Before kids eat, pray: **God, thanks for making us special. Help us remember how much you love us and how special that makes us. Amen.**

Have children take the pictures and snowflakes home, or post them on a bulletin board titled "God's Special Creations."

by Karen M. Ball

GOD SAYS I'M SPECIAL

Just like snowflakes are
unique and one of a kind . . .

I'm one of a kind!

(Genesis 1:31)

PART 2:
A LIVELY LOOK
at MY
RELATIONSHIPS

FRIENDS FOREVER

As preschool children progress, their social development changes. According to Mary Irene Flanagan, author of the *Preschool Handbook*, 3-year-olds like being with other children but still like to play alone. Four-year-olds begin to show a growing interest in doing things with other children. And by the time children turn 5, they seek affection from their peers and like to play in small groups.

As preschool children develop socially, they need to understand the importance of friendship. Use this lesson to help preschoolers learn how to be a friend.

A POWERFUL PURPOSE

Preschool children will learn that everybody can be a friend.

A LOOK AT THE LESSON

1. Bean Bag Catch (up to 6 minutes)
2. Good News About Friends (up to 4 minutes)
3. Friendship Sing-Along (up to 2 minutes)
4. A Whale of a Friend (up to 5 minutes)
5. Friendship Actions (up to 3 minutes)
6. Fantastic Friendship (up to 5 minutes)
7. Thumbody's Friend (up to 4 minutes)
8. Happy Faces (up to 5 minutes)
9. Cheer, Cheer, Cheerios! (up to 2 minutes)
10. Friendship Prayer (up to 1 minute)

A SPRINKLING OF SUPPLIES

Gather a Bible, crayons, paper, one bean bag, red and pink construction paper, posterboard, pennies, string, Cheerios (your choice of flavor) and juice.

THE LIVELY LESSON

1. Bean Bag Catch

(You'll need a bean bag.)

Have children sit in a circle. Give one child a bean bag and tell the child to say his or her name before saying "is a friend." The child then gently tosses the bean bag to another child in the circle who says his or her name before saying "is a friend," and tosses the bean bag to another child. For example, if Steven gets the bean bag first, he says, "Steven is a friend" and tosses it to Janie who says, "Janie is a friend," before tossing it to another child.

After playing the game for about three minutes, say: **Each one of us is a friend. And now we're going to say that the other children here are friends.**

Play the game again only change the game by having the child say the name of the person he or she tosses the bean bag to instead of his or her own name. For example, if Steven gets the bean bag first, he says, "Janie is a friend" before tossing the bean bag to her.

After the game say: **Isn't it great that we're all friends? God is happy when we're all good friends.**

2. Good News About Friends

Say: **The Bible has some good news about friends. In Proverbs 17:17 it says, "A friend loves you all the time." Now we're going to learn this Bible verse.**

Have children crouch down near the floor. Explain that they'll say the verse five times, first in a whisper and then a little louder each time. Also, each time they should stand a little more so that they're standing and shouting the verse the fifth time they say it.

3. Friendship Sing-Along

Have children sing together these words to the tune of "Skip to My Lou." Ask children to point to themselves when they refer to themselves in the song and point to another child when singing "you." Join hands on the last line.

I'm a friend and that is true.
I'm a friend and that is true.
I'm a friend and that is true.
I'm a friend forever.

You're a friend and that is true.
You're a friend and that is true.
You're a friend and that is true.
You're a friend forever.

I'm a friend and so are you.
I'm a friend and so are you.
I'm a friend and so are you.
Let's be friends together.

4. A Whale of a Friend

(Cut out hearts from red and pink construction paper. Cut enough hearts so each child has one. Fold all the hearts in half. You'll also need crayons.)

Give the children crayons and the hearts you cut from red and pink construction paper. Be sure the hearts are folded in half so they look like whales. Tell the children to decorate their whales by adding faces. After children finish, have them exchange whales with someone in the room.

Say: **We can have a whale of a good time when we're with good friends. Now open your whales, what do you see?** (Children will see a heart.) **When we're friends, we love each other. And God wants us to be friends. Keep your whale-heart as a reminder of what good friends you have.**

5. Friendship Actions

Have children do the following actions while you read this short action story.

Everybody is a friend, and good friends stand proud. (Have children stand.)

The reason we can be proud is that God made us. Let's all shout, "Thank you for making us, God." (Have children say, "Thank you for making us, God!")

God wants us each to be a friend. And one way we can be a friend is by smiling at the people around us. (Have children smile at each other.)

And by telling other people that they're good friends. (Have children say, "You're a good friend" to the children around them.)

Friends like to be together. They clap because they're happy. (Have children clap.)

They hug each other because they like each other. (Have children hug each other.)

And they jump for joy because everybody's a friend. (Have children jump.)

All this is because God made us. Let's thank God again for making us and let's clap too! (Children say "Thanks for making us, God!" and clap at the same time.)

6. Fantastic Friendship

Have children sit. Briefly tell the story of Jonathan and David from I Samuel 19:1-6. Ask: **How was Jonathan a good friend to David?**

Say: **We're going to repeat the Bible verse in Proverbs about friendship. I'll start out the sentence, and if you remember how it ends, jump up and finish the sentence.** Say:

A friend loves you all the _____.

Continue to repeat the verse by leaving out one more word at the end of each line until the children know the verse well.

7. Thumbody's Friend

Have children hold their thumbs up. Tell them to run around the room and press their thumbs against other children's thumbs and say, "I'm thumbody's friend, and that thumbody is you!"

Let the children continue this exercise until they've each interacted with most of the other children.

8. Happy Faces

(Tape pennies and string on a piece of posterboard as shown in the "Penny Face" diagram. The pennies form the eyes and noses, the string forms the face outlines and smiles.)

Give each child a piece of paper and crayon. Have children each take

PENNY FACE

turns putting their piece of paper on your posterboard items and rubbing gently with their crayons until the outlines and textures appear. Ask:

● **What do you see?**
● **Why are these faces happy?**

Say: **On our papers we see two happy faces. This is how friends look when they are together. They smile a lot. They laugh. They're happy. We can be happy like this when we're with our friends.**

9. Cheer, Cheer, Cheerios!

(You'll need Cheerios [your choice of flavor] and juice.)

Say: **Because we're happy that we have friends and that each one of us is a good friend, let's cheer three times! Then after we cheer three times, let's celebrate being friends by eating some Cheerios.**

Together cheer three times. Then serve a snack of Cheerios and juice.

10. Friendship Prayer

Ask the children to stand in a circle and link arms. Say: **God wants us to love each other and be friends. Each one of you is special, and you're each a good friend. Now let's bow our heads and pray.**

Pray: **God, help us to love each other and be good friends. Amen.**

by Jolene L. Roehlkepartain

BEING KIND

Kindness is a quality many children don't have naturally. Selfishness is human nature; kindness is a fruit of the Spirit. "But the Spirit gives love, joy, peace, patience, kindness, goodness, faithfulness, gentleness, self-control," (Galatians 5:22).

When preschoolers see kindness modeled by families, friends and teachers, they can imitate the examples.

Use this lesson to model kindness to young children. Help them learn and use that important quality in their lives.

A POWERFUL PURPOSE

Preschool children will understand the importance of kindness and practice it.

A LOOK AT THE LESSON

1. A Unique Guest (up to 5 minutes)
2. Be Kind to Animals
   (up to 4 minutes)
3. Be Kind to Others
   (up to 6 minutes)
4. Mobile Stories (up to 6 minutes)
5. Practice Time (up to 4 minutes)
6. Snack Exchange
   (up to 5 minutes)
7. Partner Cleanup
   (up to 3 minutes)
8. Kindness Prayer
   (up to 2 minutes)

A SPRINKLING OF SUPPLIES

Gather a Bible, crayons, photocopies of the handout, scissors, a hole punch, yarn, bananas, juice, cups, napkins, a trash can, and an animal such as a dog, cat or rabbit. You'll also need a wire clothes hanger for each child.

THE LIVELY LESSON

1. A Unique Guest

(Bring a small animal—a dog, cat or rabbit—for children to pet. Choose a calm animal that won't get scared around the children, possibly hurting them.)

As children arrive, gather in a circle. Show them the animal and let them take turns petting it. Show children how to pet the animal—softly, gently stroking it. Explain to children that softly petting the animal is a way to show kindness to it.

Let everyone have a chance to show kindness to one of God's creations.

Then have someone take the animal back to its home.

2. Be Kind to Animals

Praise the children for being kind to the animal. Ask:

● **Who made animals?**
● **Why is it important that we're nice to them?**
● **Does anyone have pets at home?**

● **How can we be kind to animals?**

Allow time for kids to talk about being kind to animals by feeding them regularly, giving them plenty to drink, brushing them and playing with them. Say: **God made the animals. He wants us to be kind to them.**

3. Be Kind to Others

(For each child, you'll need crayons and a photocopy of the "Kind Friends" handout. Cut out the four pictures on the handout. You'll also need a Bible.)

Say: **God made the animals, and God also made you. God is happy when we're kind to animals. God is also happy when we're kind to each other. God wants us to be kind to others just like we were kind to the animal.**

Pass out crayons and the first picture from the "Kind Friends" handout. Briefly explain how Matthew 9:1-2, 6-8 tells us about people who were kind to their friend who couldn't walk. The friends took the paralyzed man to Jesus so Jesus could help him walk. Allow kids to color the picture.

Distribute the second picture and tell how Jesus responded to these friends' faith. He helped the paralyzed man walk.

Give kids the third picture and explain to children that everyone was excited because Jesus healed the man.

After children have colored the third picture, pass out the final square and read it to the kids: **Thank you, Jesus, for the kindness of friends.**

Let children color this final square.

4. Mobile Stories

(You'll need a hole punch. For each child, you'll need a wire clothes hanger and four pieces of yarn varying in length from 6 to 12 inches.)

Punch a hole in each picture and tie a piece of yarn to it. Attach the four pictures to a wire clothes hanger.

After kids' mobiles are finished, help them review the story. Point to the pictures and let kids tell you the story by describing the picture. Ask:

● **Who made us?**

● **Why do you think we should be kind to each other?**

● **How can we be kind to each other?**

Hang the mobile stories around the room so kids can see kindness throughout the rest of this lesson.

5. Practice Time

Lead kids in making a one-two rhythm by patting their knees, then clapping their hands. Chant these words together:

Practice time.
Practice time.
Time to practice
Being kind.

Form pairs by having kids face a person who's sitting close to them. Say: **We're going to practice being nice to each other. Shake your partner's hand and say: "I like you. You're my friend."**

Allow 30 seconds for this hand-shaking time.

Say: **Now, tell your partner one thing you really like about him or her. For example: "I really like your smile. It makes me feel good." Or "I really like your laugh. It makes me happy."**

You may need to help children who have trouble thinking of something. Afterward, praise the children for being kind to each other.

KIND FRIENDS

These are scenes from the story in Matthew 9:1-2, 6-8

Friends carrying the lame man.

Jesus healing the man.

KIND FRIENDS

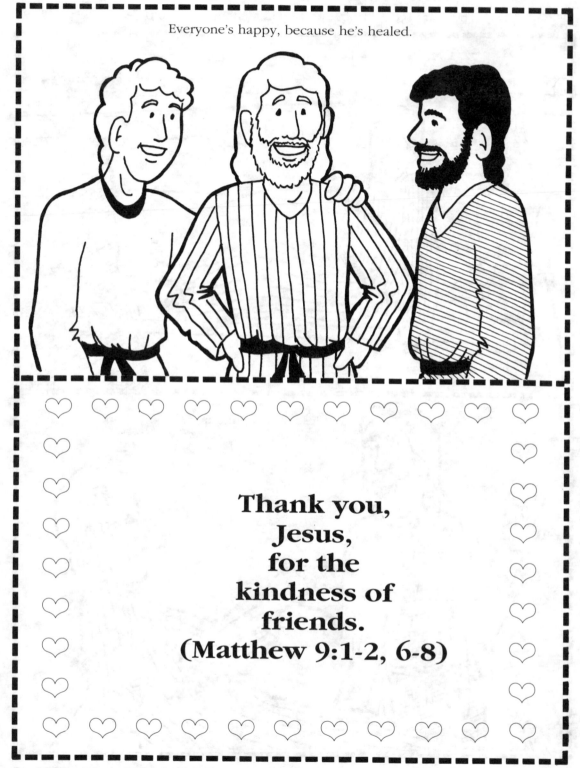

Everyone's happy, because he's healed.

Thank you, Jesus, for the kindness of friends. (Matthew 9:1-2, 6-8)

6. Snack Exchange

(For each child, you'll need a banana, cup of juice and a napkin. Slice each banana at the stem to make them easier for children to peel.)

Keep pairs from the last activity. Pass out a banana to every child. Instruct kids each to give their banana to their partner and say: "This banana is for you. Eat and enjoy."

Praise the children for their kindness in giving each other their fruit. Allow time for them to eat.

Pour juice into a small cup for each child. Again, encourage children each to give their drink to their partner. Praise them as they successfully complete the exchange.

7. Partner Cleanup

(You'll need a trash can.)

Say: **You've been kind to your partners by giving them a snack. Show your kindness even more by cleaning up for them.**

Let kids gather peelings, empty cups and napkins and throw them away.

8. Kindness Prayer

Ask partners to hold hands, bow their heads and pray silently as you pray: **God, thanks for friends. Help us be kind to show your love to others. Amen.**

Let kids take home their mobiles as a reminder to be kind to others.

by Patti Chromey

LEARNING TO SHARE

Preschoolers can be possessive. It's natural for children to hold onto what they have, but sharing can be learned—through patient, diligent and consistent teaching.

Use this lesson to help kids learn to share.

A POWERFUL PURPOSE

Preschool children will hear a story about Elijah and learn how to share.

A LOOK AT THE LESSON

1. Create a Toy (up to 6 minutes)
2. Create a Clay Story
   (up to 5 minutes)
3. The Bible Skit (up to 6 minutes)
4. Sharing a Snack With Family
   (up to 5 minutes)
5. Steppingstones to Sharing
   (up to 6 minutes)
6. Share Our Gifts (up to 5 minutes)
7. I Love to Share (up to 4 minutes)
8. Share Prayer (up to 3 minutes)

A SPRINKLING OF SUPPLIES

Gather a Bible, clay, strawberry jam, butter, bread, sandwich bags, strawberry Kool-Aid or juice, cups, napkins, photocopies of handouts, yarn, hole punch and crayons.

THE LIVELY LESSON

1. Create a Toy

(You'll need clay.)
As children arrive, greet them and tell them that you're glad they came. Give every other child a handful of clay. Tell kids with clay each to share half with someone who doesn't have any.

Tell children to form the clay into the shape of a favorite toy, such as a ball or jump rope. Demonstrate with a handful of clay so kids see an example. While they're shaping their own toys, ask:

● **Did you like sharing your clay with a friend? Why or why not?**
● **What did it feel like to give clay away?**
● **What did it feel like to receive clay?**

Say: **Sometimes it's not fun to share. I really appreciate the way you worked together. It pleases God when we share the nice things he gives us.**

2. Create a Clay Story

(You'll need the completed clay toy shapes.)

As children complete their work, ask them to sit in a large circle. Say: **We're going to make up a story about sharing, using your clay figures. When I pause telling the story, we'll go around the circle and you'll hold up your clay figure and say what it is.**

Once upon a time, God blessed some children with all kinds of toys such as ... (Go around the circle and have kids name their clay toy shapes.)

One day a little girl and boy moved into town. They were very poor. They didn't have many toys. They didn't have much of anything. They didn't have . . . (Go around and have kids name toys.)

All the children of the class met the two children and decided they wanted to share their toys with them. "Here," they said. "Play with us. Play with our . . ." (Go around and have kids name toys.)

The kids shared. Everyone was happy.

3. The Bible Skit

(You'll need a Bible.)

Open your Bible to 1 Kings 17:8-16. Make sure to use a translation that's easy for the children to understand. Read the story about Elijah and the widow who shared her food.

Say: We're going to act out this Bible story. Everybody stand up. Half of you will be Elijah and the other half will be the widow. I'll tell you what to say and do.

Elijah was very hungry. (Elijah group says, "I'm very hungry.")

He saw a woman. (Elijah group and widow group wave to each other.)

Elijah asked for water. (Elijah group says: "I'm thirsty. Can I have some water?")

The widow said, "Okay." (Widow group says, "Okay" and pretends to give water.)

Elijah asked for bread. (Elijah group says, "Can I have some bread?")

The widow said, "I barely have enough for my family" (Widow group says the words.)

But she did it anyway. (Widow group says, "Okay. Here.")

And God kept the flour and oil coming and coming. (All say, "Thank you, God!")

The widow shared (Tell widow group to wave.)

With Elijah (Tell Elijah group to wave.)

And God blessed them both. (Everybody claps.)

4. Sharing a Snack With Family

(Prepare strawberry jam and butter sandwiches. Make two for each child and place each one in a sandwich bag. You'll also need strawberry Kool-Aid or juice, cups and napkins.)

Say: When the widow shared as God wanted her to, God took care of her. Often we're afraid to share our things because we're afraid we won't have them anymore. But God will always be good to us when we're kind to others and share.

Pass out the sandwiches, two for each person. Say: Eat one now and share the other with your family when you go home.

Give kids Kool-Aid or juice and enjoy eating the snacks.

5. Steppingstones to Sharing

(You'll need photocopies of the "Steppingstone to Sharing" handout.)

Tell kids they're going to learn a Bible verse about sharing. "Share what we have with others" (a paraphrase of Luke 3:11). Have kids repeat it after you until they have it memorized.

Place the paper steppingstones on the floor across an imaginary river. Have children walk across the steppingstones as they repeat the verse again.

6. Share Our Gifts

(You'll need photocopies of the "Share Our Gifts" handout, 2-foot

STEPPINGSTONE
TO SHARING

"Share what
we have
with others."
(Luke 3:11)

pieces of yarn and crayons. Cut out the bread shape from each handout and punch two holes in the top.)

Give each person crayons and a bread shape. Read the words. Ask kids to say them with you as you read them again: **God wants us to share.** The bread represents the bread the widow shared with Elijah in the Bible story.

Let them color their bread shape. Say: **You've really learned your lesson well because I see several of you sharing your crayons.**

When children finish coloring, thread a piece of yarn through the holes of each bread shape and tie it to make a necklace. Have kids share their art by exchanging with someone else.

7. I Love to Share

Ask kids to stand and join hands in a circle. Sing the following song to the tune of "Twinkle, Twinkle, Little Star." Go through the song slowly and teach the words and actions. Repeat it several times.

How I, how I love to share (Walk to the middle of the circle.)

With my neighbors everywhere. (Walk out.)

It pleases Jesus when I do. (Kids point up.)

It makes us happy, me and you. (Kids shake hands with someone and join hands in a circle again.)

How I, how I love to share (Walk to the middle of the circle.)

With my neighbors everywhere. (Walk out.)

8. Share Prayer

(You'll need the paper stepping-stones with Luke 3:11 on them.)

Ask children to stay in the circle, holding hands. Pray: **Dear God, thank you for your gifts. Help us share what we have with others. Amen.**

Place the paper steppingstones with the Bible verse on them, leading up to the door. As kids start to leave, have them walk along each step and say the words, "Share what we have with others!" Then have kids each pick one up to take with them.

by Ray and Cindy Peppers

SHARE OUR GIFTS

God wants us to share.

DON'T FIGHT!

Many of today's TV shows and movies teach that the one who's strongest is best. The person who gets in the last "hit" is the winner. But Jesus says to turn the other cheek. He says if someone wants your shirt, give him your coat too. Again and again we see Jesus making peace among would-be fighters.

Use this lesson to help young children learn more about hurting others and fighting. God wants us to bring peace, not harm, to others.

A POWERFUL PURPOSE

Preschool children will learn to be peacemakers instead of fighters.

A LOOK AT THE LESSON

1. Be a Friend (up to 6 minutes)
2. It's Mine (up to 4 minutes)
3. Jesus Tells Us (up to 4 minutes)
4. Act Out a Story (up to 6 minutes)
5. Puppet Productions
   (up to 6 minutes)
6. Puppet Performance
   (up to 6 minutes)
7. A Snack Like David's
   (up to 4 minutes)
8. Blessed Are the Peacemakers
   (up to 4 minutes)

A SPRINKLING OF SUPPLIES

Gather a Bible, crayons, paper plates, Popsicle sticks, glue, tables, fresh fruit, water, cups and napkins.

THE LIVELY LESSON

1. Be a Friend

As kids enter the room, gather them in a line for an opening game. With one of the taller kids, form a "bridge": Face each other, grab each other's hands, and hold them up high in an arch. Ask children to travel under the bridge, around you and back under the bridge while you sing this song to the tune of "London Bridge":

Fighting, fighting all the time,
All the time,
All the time,
Fighting, fighting all the time,
Be a friend (Name).

On the words "Be a friend (Name)," say the child's name who's under the bridge at that time, and bring your clasped arms down around him or her. Rock the child back and forth as you sing:

Never, never hurt others,
Hurt others,
Hurt others,
Never, never hurt others,
Be a friend (Name).

Now let the person you just rocked switch places with the person who was helping you form a bridge. Continue until everyone gets a turn being rocked. Encourage all kids to sing with you.

2. It's Mine

(You'll need one crayon for every two people. You'll also need a Bible.)

Say: **We're going to talk about fighting and hurting each other. We're going to discover better, peaceful ways to solve problems instead of hurtful ways of doing it.**

Form pairs. Give every pair a crayon and ask the partners to both hold it. On the count of three, have them pretend to fight over the crayon. One says, "It's mine," and pulls it toward himself; the other says, "No! It's mine," and pulls it toward herself. Have them keep going back and forth like this until you say "Stop."

After children have pretended awhile, tell them to stop, then ask:

● **How did it feel to fight over a crayon?**

● **Have you fought over toys or clothes or food before? When?**

● **Instead of fighting over the crayon, how could we solve the problem?**

Say: **One way to solve that kind of problem is to share. Take turns. Jesus wants us to think of others and help them. Give. Listen to his advice.**

Read Luke 6:29: "If anyone slaps you on your cheek, let him slap the other cheek too. If someone takes your coat, do not stop him from taking your shirt."

In other words, don't fight.

Ask: **What are some things that make you so mad you want to fight?** Listen for things such as bullies, people not sharing toys, hitting, not playing fair.

Ask children about ways to handle the situations. Help them think of positive reactions.

3. Jesus Tells Us

Sing this song to the tune of "Mary Had a Little Lamb." Sing through the two verses several times to help kids learn it.

**If a person makes you mad,
Makes you mad,
Makes you mad,
If a person makes you mad,
Turn the other cheek.**

**Jesus tells us do not fight,
Do not fight,
Do not fight,
Jesus tells us do not fight,
Be a peacemaker.**

Tell kids that a peacemaker is someone who loves other people and doesn't fight.

4. Act Out a Story

Say: **We're going to hear a Bible story about David and King Saul. David had a chance to fight, but he didn't. I'll say some words and do some actions, you repeat the words and the actions.**

This story is from 1 Samuel 26.

Saul was a king. (Stand proud.)

David was a brave young man. (Arm across chest, look brave.)

King Saul was jealous and wanted to kill David. (Look jealous.)

David feared for his life, so he ran. (Run in place.)

King Saul went looking for David. (Hand above eyes and look.)

One night while King Saul was sleeping, (Fold hands by cheek, close eyes and say, "Z-z-z-z-z-z-z.")

David quietly came up to him. (Tiptoe in place, put finger to lips and say, "Sh-h-h-h-h-h.")

David could have killed King Saul. (Raise arm as if you're going to strike.)

But he didn't. (Drop arm and shake head.)

He took Saul's spear and water

jug (Pretend to lift one in each hand.)

And left. (Tiptoe quietly.)

He then yelled at the King's guard away at a safe distance, "Wake up!" (Cup hands around mouth and yell words.)

"You weren't doing your job!" (Say the words loudly.)

"I could have killed King Saul!" (Say the words loudly.)

"But I didn't!" (Say the words loudly.)

David threw down King Saul's spear and water jug to prove it. (Pretend to throw down each item.)

King Saul heard this (Hand to ear.)

And said, "May you be blessed David." (Say the words loudly.)

"God is with you." (Point up.)

And King Saul went back home. (Walk in place.)

Say: **David was a peacemaker. He could have fought, but he didn't.**

5. Puppet Productions

(Make puppets by gluing a Popsicle stick handle on the back of each paper plate, make two for each child. You'll also need crayons.)

Say: **Now we're going to make puppets and perform David's story again.**

Give kids each two paper plate puppets and crayons. Tell them to design a David puppet and a King Saul puppet. You design a couple puppets along with them so they can see examples.

6. Puppet Performance

(You'll need the completed puppets and a puppet stage. Make a stage by turning a table on its side. Use as many tables as you can so half the class can perform at a time.)

Say: **Hold up your King Saul puppets. They look great! Everybody say "Hi, King Saul!" Now hold up your David puppets. They look great too! Everybody say "Hi, David!"**

Have half of the class find a place behind the puppet stage; the other half of the class will be the audience. Say: **Lights! Cameras! Action!** Read the story again, only this time have the puppets perform.

Then switch and let the other half of the class perform while the others watch.

7. A Snack Like David's

(You'll need fresh fruit, water, cups and napkins.)

Ask kids what they think David might have eaten while he was running from Saul. He had to live in the desert and in the mountains. Some suggestions are wild game, nuts, seeds, berries, and lots of water for his thirst. Serve children fresh fruit and water.

Say: **David couldn't be at his house eating home-cooked meals while Saul was chasing him, so he had to eat a lot of these other things. David must have thanked God even for what he had. Let's thank God for these snacks and for David who showed us not to fight. There are better ways to solve problems.**

Pray as a group. Have kids repeat each line after you:

Come, Lord Jesus,
Help us find
Ways that are peaceful,
Thoughtful, kind.
When we feel
We want to fight,
Help us stop

With your power and might.
Amen.

8. Blessed Are the Peacemakers

(Teach Matthew 5:9 as the memory verse. Sing the following words to the tune of "Jesus Loves Me."

Blessed are the peacemakers,
Blessed are the peacemakers,
Blessed are the peacemakers,
Blessed are the peacemakers.

Let's stop our fighting,
Let's stop our fighting,
Let's stop our fighting
And do what God would do.

Let children take their puppets home and perform the David and Saul story for their family.

by Ray and Cindy Peppers

LEND A HELPING HAND

Preschool children love to help. They enjoy getting along with others and want to please. Helping other people encourages interaction, reinforces biblical values and helps model Christian behavior.

Use this lesson to teach preschoolers about helping. Give them a chance to be kind to each other.

A POWERFUL PURPOSE

Preschool children will hear a Bible story about the good Samaritan and practice helping others.

A LOOK AT THE LESSON

1. Fast First Aid (up to 5 minutes)
2. The Good Samaritan
   (up to 3 minutes)
3. Toss a Tale (up to 5 minutes)
4. Create a Card (up to 6 minutes)
5. Repeat-After-Me Prayer
   (up to 3 minutes)
6. Sugar Cookie Snack
   (up to 6 minutes)
7. Band-Aid Reminder
   (up to 4 minutes)
8. Mail a Card (up to 3 minutes)

A SPRINKLING OF SUPPLIES

Gather a doll, Band-Aid bandages, an elastic bandage, wet washcloths, towels, a Bible, pictures of the good Samaritan story, a bean bag, tempera paints, foil pans, old shirts or aprons, cookie cutters, photocopies of the handout, napkins, cups, milk, a marker, half-page-size envelopes, stamps, and sugar cookies.

THE LIVELY LESSON

1. Fast First Aid

(Place the following supplies on a table: a doll, Band-Aid bandages, an elastic bandage, wet washcloths, towels.)

Welcome children and tell them they're going to learn about helping others. Gather around the table with the doll and first aid supplies on it. Say: **Pretend this doll is a little child and she's just been badly hurt. What could you use to help her feel better?**

Let children wipe the doll with wet washcloths, dry her off, put Band-Aid bandages on injuries, and wrap an arm or leg with the bandage. Then ask:

● **How did we help this doll?**
● **Have you ever helped someone? When?**
● **How does it make you feel when you help someone?**

2. The Good Samaritan

(You'll need a Bible.)

Say: **Jesus told stories of how other people were helpers too. Let's read about a helper called the good Samaritan. He was a man from a country called Samaria.**

Read the story from Luke 10:30-37 in

a children's Bible. Pause after each verse. Have kids say, "Jesus wants us to help" and clap as they say each word.

3. Toss a Tale

(You'll need a bean bag and pictures of the good Samaritan story.)

Tell kids they're going to play a game to help them remember the story. Lay the pictures on the floor. Have children take turns tossing the bean bag on one of the pictures and telling the part of the story depicted. You go first so they see how to do it; then let them take turns tossing a tale.

For example, if a bean bag lands on a picture of a hurt man on a donkey, a child may tell about how the good Samaritan put the hurt man on his donkey and took him to get help.

4. Create a Card

(Prepare a table with card-making supplies such as tempera paint in foil pans, cookie cutters, and old shirts or aprons. Photocopy the "Create a Card" handout. Ask your pastor about congregation members who are ill or who need extra prayers and encouragement. Make a list of their names and addresses.)

Say: **Today we're going to be God's helpers too. We're going to help people feel better. We're going to make get-well cards for people who are sick or need some cheering up.**

Help children cover their good clothes with old shirts or aprons. Give them each a handout. Read the words: **God loves you so much. He's watching over you.** Fold the cards with the words inside. Have kids decorate the blank outside of the card.

Show kids how to dip a cookie cutter in the paint, lift it out and "stamp" the handout. Tell them to design their cards any way they want—repeat the same shape with different colors or use different shapes and overlap prints.

Complete the cards, then wash hands and clean up.

5. Repeat-After-Me Prayer

While cards are drying, ask kids to pray by repeating each line you say and the actions you do.

Dear God, (Fold hands.)

We are your helpers. (Raise hands to heaven.)

Let us be good helpers this week (Put hands on shoulders.)

To all of those people around us. (Motion arms all around.)

Amen. (Fold hands.)

6. Sugar Cookie Snack

(You'll need napkins, cups, milk and cookies you made before the lesson from the cookie cutters used for the art project.)

Follow the prayer with a snack of milk and sugar cookies. Ask kids if the shapes look familiar to them. As they munch on their cookies, let them go by the table and look at the card designs.

7. Band-Aid Reminder

(You'll need Band-Aid bandages and a marker.)

Gather kids in a circle and ask:

● **Who are God's helpers?** (Name each child in the class.)

● **How do we help others?**

To help remind them of today's lesson and the fact that they are God's helpers, write "Luke 10:30-37" on a Band-Aid, for each child. Place the Band-Aids on the backs of kids' hands.

Tell kids that Luke 10:30-37 is the place in the Bible that tells about God's helper, the good Samaritan. Encourage kids to ask a parent to read the story again at home.

8. Mail a Card

(Address envelopes for the congregation members on your list. Mark an X on each envelope where kids are to stick a stamp.)

Check to see if the get-well cards are dry. If they are, let kids each place their card in an envelope and stick a stamp in the corner over the X. Let them take their cards home to mail. Or, if time allows, take the entire class to a nearby mailbox and let kids mail their cards.

by Nanette Goings

CREATE A CARD

fold

inside of card

How Do You Feel?

Young children aren't yet equipped with appropriate outlets for emotions and often express them in negative ways. They're confused by reactions around them and are searching for a way to help others understand how they feel.

It's okay to feel happy, sad, angry, lonely and scared. God knows how children feel and can help them deal with their emotions. But other people around them need to know about those emotions as well. If children hit, scream or cry, others may not understand. But, if children learn to use words to express their feelings, others will better be able to help.

Use this lesson to give children opportunities to explore their emotions and express them to others.

A POWERFUL PURPOSE

Preschool children will learn to use words to tell family and friends how they feel.

A LOOK AT THE LESSON

1. If You're Happy
   (up to 6 minutes)
2. Guess the Feelings
   (up to 6 minutes)
3. Cookie Faces (up to 5 minutes)
4. Finger Painting Feelings
   (up to 6 minutes)
5. March Around the Feelings
   (up to 6 minutes)
6. Feel the Feeling (up to 6 minutes)
7. Sandpaper Faces
   (up to 6 minutes)
8. Lip-Smacking Snack Time
   (up to 5 minutes)

A SPRINKLING OF SUPPLIES

Gather a Bible, a marker, old shirts or aprons, magazines, cookie dough, raisins and red hot candy, sandwich bags, wax paper, whipped topping, food coloring, paper plates, a tape of lively music, a tape player, sandpaper, red yarn, crayons and a scarf for each child.

THE LIVELY LESSON

1. If You're Happy

Welcome the children, then lead them in singing the traditional song "If You're Happy and You Know It."

After the song, gather the children in front of you and teach this action poem:

Sometimes I feel happy. (Show happy face.)

Sometimes I feel sad. (Show sad face.)

Sometimes I feel sleepy. (Yawn.)

And sometimes I feel mad. (Show angry face.)

But no matter how I'm feeling, (Shrug shoulders.)

God helps me to be strong, (Show muscles.)

And to tell about my feelings (Point to mouth.)

All day long. (Clap each word.)

Say: **God made you with all kinds**

of feelings inside. **It's okay to feel happy, sad, scared, lonely and even mad. But God wants us to share our feelings and not keep them locked up inside. We know he'll help us understand how we feel and give us the words to tell others too. He tells us in the Bible that he'll be there to help us when we need him. He can help us not feel sad, scared, lonely or mad when we trust him to take care of us.**

Read Hebrews 13:6: "I will not be afraid because the Lord is my helper."

Say: **Because the Lord is our helper, he'll help us get rid of the feelings that bother us if we tell him about them.**

2. Guess the Feelings

(Clip pictures from magazines that show people expressing diverse emotions such as fear, anger, happiness and worry.)

Show the magazine pictures to the children and ask:

● **What do you see in this picture?**

● **What do you think is happening in this picture?**

● **How do you think this person feels?**

● **How do you know the person feels this way?**

● **Have you ever felt this way? When?**

Throughout the discussion, emphasize that other people share the same emotions the children do. God knows how we feel, and other people will understand our feelings too.

Throughout the discussion, encourage language such as, "I feel angry when . . ." or "I feel sad when . . ." This way, the children can practice verbalizing their feelings within a safe environment.

3. Cookie Faces

(Provide sliced refrigerator cookie dough, raisins and red hot candies.)

Give children each two slices of cookie dough. Encourage them to use the raisins and red hot candies to make a face on each cookie. Direct them to make their cookie faces each express a feeling.

Ask kids to tell the feeling they're giving each of their two cookies. While you continue with the lesson, have an adult helper bake the cookies.

4. Finger Painting Feelings

(You'll need wax paper, whipped topping with food coloring mixed in, and old shirts or aprons.)

Cover kids' good clothes with old shirts or aprons. Give kids each a large piece of waxed paper and have them sit at the table. On each piece of waxed paper place a small mound of whipped topping. Encourage the children to use their fingers and hands to spread the whipped cream out on the paper. (It's okay if they taste a little bit!)

Invite children to draw faces showing different emotions. Say: **Draw how you feel when:**

● **someone gives you a candy bar.**

● **someone sneaks up behind you and yells "Boo!"**

● **you trip and fall down, scraping your knee on the sidewalk.**

Encourage children to continue drawing other emotions and talking about the situations. Remind them that God knows how they feel and that they can tell others too.

Use water and towels to clean up in the room, or take children to a restroom.

5. March Around the Feelings

(On paper plates draw various faces depicting a variety of feelings. Make several of each kind so you'll have one for each child. You'll also need a tape of lively music and a tape player.)

Place the paper plate faces in a circle on the floor. Say: **Look at all the paper faces on the floor. They show all kinds of feelings such as happiness, sadness and anger. I'll play some music and you march around outside the circle of faces. When the music stops, you stop. Look at the plate in front of you and pretend to feel that way. Then we'll talk about that feeling.**

Continue the game, playing music and stopping until everyone has had an opportunity to talk about several feelings.

6. Feel the Feelings

(Each child will need a scarf or piece of silky material. Chiffon scarves work best and can be found at second-hand stores.)

Give children each a scarf or piece of silky material. Tell them to practice twirling their scarves all around them in a happy way and quietly repeat the phrase, "Sometimes I feel happy, happy, happy." Then, tell them to stop, pretend to be angry and to wad the scarf into a ball. Direct them to throw the scarf into the air as they repeat the phrase, "Sometimes I feel angry, angry, angry." They can catch the scarves and try again until you direct them to resume moving in a happy way.

Alternate feelings and actions as time and interest permit. Remember to repeat the phrases so children can hear how to verbalize these feelings.

Say: **See how easy it is to talk about feelings? We need to remember to let God and others know how we feel.**

7. Sandpaper Faces

(Each child will need crayons, a 3-inch piece of red yarn and a 5-inch circle that has been cut from sandpaper.)

Give children each a sandpaper circle. Direct them to use crayons to make eyes and a nose. Give children each a 3-inch piece of red yarn to be used as a mouth. The yarn will stick to the sandpaper and can be changed from a smile to a frown to an angry face.

Give children an opportunity to decide which emotion they want their sandpaper face to display and to show it to others. Let children tell about a time they experienced that emotion. Praise them for their efforts and remind them how important it is to tell God and others how they feel when they experience similar situations.

8. Lip-Smacking Snack Time

(You'll need the baked cookies, sandwich bags and photocopies of the handout.)

Let kids each eat one cookie they made. Talk about the feelings depicted.

Close by paraphrasing Hebrews 13:6: **(Name) will not be afraid because the Lord is (Name)'s helper.** (Say this to each child, using his or her name.)

Say: **When we tell God about our fears or our other feelings, he'll help us handle them in a good way.**

Let kids each take home their other cookie in a sandwich bag. Attach the "Cookie Face" handout. Write each child's name in the blanks provided on the handout.

Read the note aloud to kids: **Hi! I'm a cookie face. (Name) made me. Ask (Name) to tell you how I feel.**

Say: **Be sure you tell your family what kind of face and feeling you designed for your cookie. Remember God is your helper. He'll help you handle all your feelings in a good way.**

by Jane P. Wilke

COOKIE FACE

Hi! I'm a cookie face.

_____ made me.

Ask _____ to tell

you how I feel.

COOKIE FACE

Hi! I'm a cookie face.

_____ made me.

Ask _____ to tell

you how I feel.

CARING FOR GOD'S WORLD

Children this age are naturally enthusiastic about the world around them. Animals, trees, colors, shapes, smells—everything in nature is a source of great delight.

Use this lesson as an adventure for all of the senses. Focus the children's attention on how things feel (the sun on their faces), smell (flowers), taste (things to eat), sound (birds and animals), and look (all creation around them). Use this time to help children discover the wonders of God's world and to recognize how sad we would be if we were to lose any of it.

A POWERFUL PURPOSE

Preschool children will learn practical ways to care for God's creation.

A LOOK AT THE LESSON

1. Puzzles—Putting It Together (up to 6 minutes)
2. Experience God's Creation (up to 6 minutes)
3. Tear a Photo (up to 5 minutes)
4. Let's Make a World (up to 4 minutes)
5. Something's Missing (up to 4 minutes)
6. Care Walk (up to 6 minutes)
7. Earth Patrol (up to 5 minutes)
8. Bird Feeders (up to 4 minutes)

A SPRINKLING OF SUPPLIES

Gather a Bible, several simple puzzles with nature or animal pictures on them, magazines, catalogs, newsprint, tape, safety pins, recycled paper, crayons, salted peanuts in the shells, yarn, fruit and photocopies of the handouts.

THE LIVELY LESSON

1. Puzzles—Putting It Together

(You'll need several simple puzzles with nature or animal pictures on them.)

Place the puzzles around on the floor. As children enter the room, invite them to put the puzzles together. Encourage kids to work together and cooperate to complete the pictures.

2. Experience God's Creation

(Do this activity outdoors. In case of bad weather, prepare an indoor nature walk. Tape pictures of flowers, sun, streams and animals on walls in the hall or various rooms.)

Say: **Today we're going to take a nature walk and experience all of God's creation. We're going to see** (point to your eyes and have kids each point to their eyes), **hear** (point to your ears and have kids each point to their ears), **smell,** (point to your nose and have kids each point to their nose), **taste** (point to your mouth and have kids each point to their mouth), and **feel** (wiggle your fingers and have kids each wiggle their fingers) **God's wonderful creation.**

Go outside and:
● See the clouds, sun, trees and seasonal gifts such as flowers.
● Hear the birds, insects and wind.
● Smell the flowers and trees.
● Taste a blade of grass or a gulp of fresh air.
● Feel rough tree bark, smooth rocks and the cool grass beneath your feet.

3. Tear a Photo

(You'll need magazines and catalogs.)

When you come back to the room, pass out the magazines and catalogs. Ask children what they liked best about the nature walk. Ask them to find pictures of what they liked and tear them out. Remember everything you saw, heard, smelled, tasted and felt.

4. Let's Make a World

(Draw a large circle on a piece of newsprint and tape it to the wall. You also will need the pictures from the last activity.)

Say: **Our world is a beautiful place. God created it with all kinds of wonderful things! Let's make a picture of our world and put on it all the things we liked from our walk.**

Ask children to bring up the items they tore out and lightly tape them in the circle. Try to include a wide variety of pictures. When you're done, stand back, look at the world, and have everyone say, "What a wonderful world!"

5. Something's Missing

Say: **God made the things we've put into our world. What would**

our world be like without them?

Start taking photos off, one by one. After removing each one, ask children: **How would you feel if (flowers, clouds, animals, water) weren't in our world any more?**

When you've taken everything off, ask: **If all of these wonderful gifts were gone, what would the world be like?**

Listen to children's responses such as empty, ugly, wouldn't smell as good.

6. Care Walk

(You'll need photocopies of the "What Can I Do?" handout.)

Read Genesis 1:26: **"And let (human beings) rule over the fish in the sea and the birds in the sky. Let them rule over the tame animals, over all the earth and over all the small crawling animals on the earth."** Say: **Like a parent takes care of a child he or she "rules over," we need to take care of our world.**

After you read from the Bible, have kids stand and say, "Let's take care of God's creation!"

Say: **There are some simple things we can do to help take care of our earth. Follow me and I'll show you.**

Take children on a walking tour to show the ideas on the "What Can I Do?" handout. For example, lead kids to a light switch and read: **Turn off the lights when you leave a room.** Lead them to a water faucet and read: **Don't run the water when brushing your teeth.**

After your Care Walk, return to the room. Give kids each a photocopy of the "What Can I Do?" handout. Say: **Take this list home and show it to**

WHAT CAN I DO?

1. Turn off the lights when you leave a room.

2. Don't run the water when brushing your teeth. Just turn it on to wet your brush and to rinse it off.

3. Put a plastic jug filled with water in your toilet's tank so it doesn't use as much water.

4. Use a cloth towel instead of a paper towel to dry your hands.

5. Paint and draw on recycled paper.

6. Set dry bread out in your yard for the birds to eat.

7. Throw trash in trash cans, not on the ground.

8. Recycle! Newspapers, cans, bottles, plastic, cereal boxes, aluminum foil—all can be recycled.

9. Pick up litter when you see it.

10. Cut the plastic rings that come on six-packs before you throw them in the trash. Small animals foraging through local dump sites have caught their necks in the rings.

11. Check with your local zoo to see if they have an adopt-an-animal program. Help care for all of God's creation.

your mom or dad. Ask your mom or dad to help you do at least one of these things during the next week.

7. Earth Patrol

(You'll need photocopies of the "Earth Patrol" handout. If possible, photocopy them on recycled paper. Cut out the badges. You'll also need safety pins and crayons.)

Give children each a badge and crayons. Read the words: **"Earth Patrol."** Let children color the badges. When you pin a finished badge to each child, say: **I now commission you to Earth Patrol. It's your job to keep watch and take care of the earth.**

After everyone has been commissioned, pray: **Father, thank you for this wonderful, beautiful world you have given us. Help us not to hurt it any more. Help us learn how to take care of it. Amen.**

8. Bird Feeders

(You'll need unsalted peanuts still in their shells and 10-inch pieces of yarn.)

Say: **One thing we all can do is help take care of the wild animals in our own yards. We're going to make bird feeders to hang in our yards. This way the birds who come to visit our houses will have some good things to eat.**

A helper could make this activity move more quickly.

Give each child a handful of salted peanuts still in their shells, and some yarn. Help them tie the peanuts to the yarn, and then tie the ends of the yarn together. Have kids each take their bird feeder home and hang it from a tree branch in their yard. The birds will find it.

Say: **Another one of God's creations we have to take care of is ourselves. One way to do this is to eat healthful foods.**

Serve fruit to God's great creation of kids.

by Karen M. Ball

PART 3:
A LIVELY LOOK AT MY FAITH

WHO IS GOD?

Preschoolers are beginning to form their ideas about who God is. Some view God as a loving parent. Others think of him as a grandfather-type. And others think of him as one who doesn't like them to do certain things.

Preschoolers need their questions about God answered simply and truthfully. Use this lesson to help your preschoolers learn about God, and how he loved us so much he sent us his son, Jesus.

A POWERFUL PURPOSE

Preschool children will learn about God and how much he loves them.

A LOOK AT THE LESSON

1. Color Their World
   (up to 5 minutes)
2. The Bible Tells Me So
   (up to 3 minutes)
3. Jesus Loves Me (up to 3 minutes)
4. Hugs of Love (up to 4 minutes)
5. He Gave Us Us (up to 3 minutes)
6. Animals for Us (up to 4 minutes)
7. A Heart for God (up to 5 minutes)
8. Love Prayer (up to 3 minutes)

A SPRINKLING OF SUPPLIES

Gather crayons, red construction paper, glue, a Bible, animal crackers, milk, cups and photocopies of the handouts.

THE LIVELY LESSON

1. Color Their World

(For each child, you'll need crayons and a photocopy of the "God Made the World" handout.)

Welcome the children as they arrive. Give them each a photocopy of the "God Made the World" handout and crayons. Have them color the items on the page.

After everyone has had a chance to color, tell the kids they're going to learn about God today. Ask:

● **Who made the things you just colored?**

● **Why did God make them?**

Say: **We know God loves us, and one of the reasons we know that is that he made wonderful flowers, trees and animals and gave them to us to enjoy.**

2. The Bible Tells Me So

Say: **Another reason we know God loves us is because the Bible tells us that he does.**

Help kids memorize this Bible verse: "Love comes from God" (1 John 4:7). Use motions to convey the words to the children as you say them.

Love (Wrap your arms around yourself.)

Comes (Motion with your hand as if signaling someone to come to you.)

From God. (Point up.)

Say the verse with the children three or four times. Have them stand and do

GOD MADE THE WORLD

the motions with you. Then let the children try saying one word by themselves as you do the motions. After a couple more times they should be able to say the verse by themselves.

3. Jesus Loves Me

Say: **The Bible tells us that love comes from God. The Bible also tells us that Jesus loves us.**

Sing "Jesus Loves Me" with the children. Use these actions.

Jesus (Point up.)
Loves (Wrap arms around yourself.)
Me; (Point to yourself.)
This I know (Point to your head.)
For the Bible (Form a Bible with your two hands.)
Tells me so. (Point to yourself.)
Little ones (Motion like your hand is placed on a little child's head.)
To him belong. (Point up.)
They are weak, (Look weak.)
But he is strong. (Form strong arms.)

Yes, (Nod head.)
Jesus (Point up.)
Loves (Wrap arms around yourself.)
Me. (Point to yourself.)
(Repeat "Yes, Jesus loves me" three times.)
The Bible (Form a Bible with your two hands.)
Tells me so. (Point to yourself.)

Then say: **To remind us that God loves us too, let's put his name in place of Jesus' name in the song.**

Sing "God Loves Me" using the same actions.

4. Hugs of Love

(You'll need a Bible.)

Say: **You know what? I love you too!** Go around and hug each child as you call him or her by name and say:

(Name), I love you. Have kids move to a different part of the room and sit down on the floor. Then say: **I hugged you to show my love for you. God doesn't come and hug us like I hugged you. But he has shown us how much he loves us by sending us his son, Jesus.**

Read a children's Bible version of John 3:16 or read this: "For God loved the world so much that he gave his only Son. God gave his Son so that whoever believes in him may not be lost, but have eternal life."

5. He Gave Us Us

Say: **Another way God shows us he loves us is by giving us bodies we can do things with. Let's stand up and thank God for the bodies he's given us.**

Have kids spread out. Tell them to repeat the words after you and follow your motions. Be sensitive to handicapped children in your class. Don't use any motions they can't do.

Thanks, God, for our hands. (Wave hands in the air.)
Thanks, God, for our feet. (Wiggle a foot in the air.)
Thanks, God, for our elbows. (Flop your elbows out at your sides.)
Thanks, God, for our knees. (March with your knees going high.)
Thanks, God, for our heads. (Roll your head around and around.)
Thanks, God, for our hips. (Wiggle your hips.)
Thanks, God, for our seats. (Sit down on the floor in a circle.)

6. Animals for Us

(You'll need animal crackers, milk and cups.)

Pass out the animal crackers and serve the milk. Before letting kids eat their crackers, go around the circle and let them describe one of their animals. Say: **Remember what we colored earlier? God loves us so much he gave us all sorts of neat things in our world. Some of those things are animals. And the milk we're drinking came from one of those animals: a cow!**

Offer a prayer thanking God for the love he showed us by giving us animals.

7. A Heart for God

(You'll need glue, crayons, red hearts cut from construction paper and the "God Loves Me" handouts. Cut the hearts so they fit over the heart shape on the handout.)

Pass out the handouts, glue and red paper hearts. Read the handout and explain where to glue the hearts. Let the children glue the hearts in place and color the letters.

Ask if anyone remembers the memory verse (Love comes from God). If no one says it, say it with the children a couple more times. Work through it until they can say it with you only doing the motions.

8. Love Prayer

(You'll need the completed "God Loves Me" handouts.)

Place the "God Loves Me" handouts in the center of the room. Ask the children to form a circle around the handouts. Say: **Look at all of these reminders of God's love. Let's pray and thank him for his love.**

Pray, thanking God for showing us his love in so many ways—his son, ourselves, animals and our world.

Then have kids place their arms on each other's shoulders and take three steps in toward the center. When they're all bunched together in a group hug, have everybody shout "God loves us!"

by Paul Woods

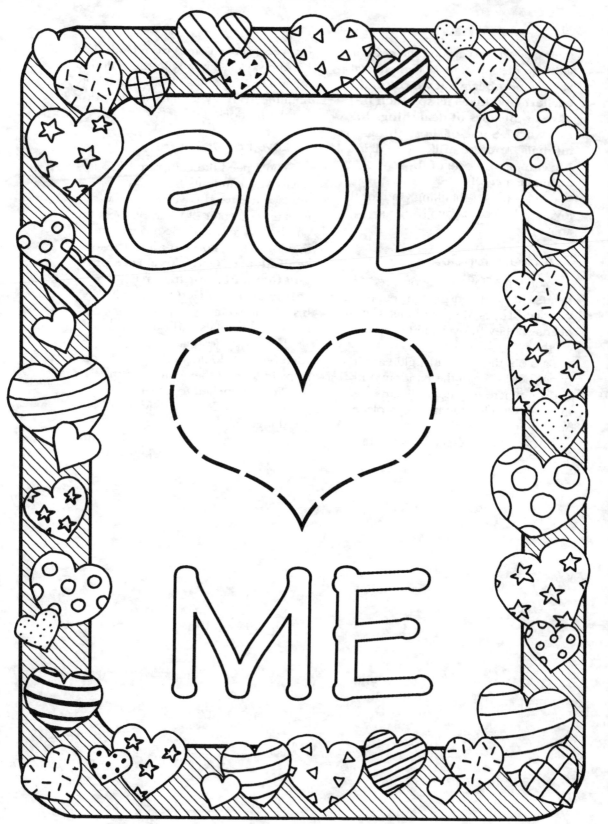

GOD ❤ ME

WHO IS JESUS?

Young children think in a concrete manner and, therefore, it's difficult for them to understand abstract concepts. They're told that Jesus loves them, however, they can't see him. To help young children understand this abstract concept, we must help them make a connection with concrete activities.

Use this lesson to repeat the theme "Jesus is with me wherever I go." Activities reiterate the theme as well as reinforce the concept.

A POWERFUL PURPOSE

Preschool children will learn that Jesus is their friend. He's with them all the time.

A LOOK AT THE LESSON

1. Jesus Is With Me
   (up to 6 minutes)
2. Crayon Resist (up to 6 minutes)
3. Shadow Screen (up to 5 minutes)
4. Listen and Do (up to 3 minutes)
5. Follow the Leader
   (up to 6 minutes)
6. Door Hanger Design
   (up to 6 minutes)
7. Jesus Hugs (up to 5 minutes)
8. Picture Pass Around
   (up to 5 minutes)

A SPRINKLING OF SUPPLIES

Gather a Bible, white crayons, white construction paper, watercolors, different-color tissue paper, glue, crayons, paintbrushes, old shirts or aprons, a tape of cheerful music, a tape player, photocopies of the handout, filmstrip or slide projector, a piece of thin white cloth, objects for the shadow screen, a picture of Jesus, twisted pretzels, apple juice, napkins and cups.

THE LIVELY LESSON

1. Jesus Is With Me

(You'll need a Bible.)

Gather children in a circle. Lead them in this action song to the tune of "The Mulberry Bush."

This is the way we swing our arms,
Swing our arms, swing our arms.
This is the way we swing our arms,
In praise to the Lord.

Sing other verses and actions such as nod our heads, clap our hands, wiggle our fingers, and march in place.

Once you've gained kids' attention and cooperation, change the song's words. Do the actions in place.

Jesus is with me when I run,
When I run, when I run.
Jesus is with me when I run,
He's with me wherever I go.

Sing other verses and actions such as when I walk, jump, skate, stretch, sleep, throw and eat.

End the activity by singing "Jesus is with me when I sit …" After kids sit, open your Bible to Matthew 28:20. Tell kids to listen quietly as you read what

Jesus said: **"I will be with you always."**

Remind kids of the song and talk briefly about the variety of times Jesus is with them throughout both day and night.

2. Crayon Resist

(You'll need a white crayon and white piece of construction paper for each child. You'll also need watercolors, paintbrushes, and old shirts or aprons.)

Cover kids' good clothes with old shirts or aprons. Give each child a white crayon and a piece of white construction paper. Instruct kids to draw a scribble design all over the paper, pressing hard with the crayon. Talk with them about how difficult it is to see the design. Then let kids paint over the entire surface of the paper with watercolors. The design will appear on the page as the crayon wax resists the paint. Share with kids that Jesus is also with us even though we can't see him.

3. Shadow Screen

(Gather a variety of objects recognizable by shape, such as a rock, pencil, cup and fork. Place them in a bag or a box. Add a cut-out shape of Jesus. Then construct a simple shadow screen by placing a thin white cloth in front of a beam of light from a filmstrip or slide projector. Nail the cloth to a wooden frame or drape it over a table.)

Set children in front of the shadow screen. Place one of the objects in the beam of light, behind the cloth. Ask kids to guess what it is by looking at the shadow. Follow this procedure with all of the shapes and end with the cut-out shape of Jesus. Say: **Just like we knew what all the other shapes were, we also knew Jesus. Jesus is with us even though we can't see him.**

If kids don't recognize Jesus, say: **Even though we didn't recognize Jesus like the other things, he's always there.**

4. Listen and Do

Ask children each to find a place on the floor, kneel down, touch their chin to their chest, and cover their closed eyes with their hands. Tiptoe quietly to a spot and say:

Peanut butter and strawberry jam,
Can you point to where I am?

Ask kids to keep their eyes closed and point to you. Tiptoe to a new location and repeat the activity several times. When finished, reinforce that the children knew you were there even though they couldn't see you. Just like we know Jesus is here even though we can't see him.

5. Follow the Leader

Gather children in a circle. Walk around them as you sing the following song to the tune of "The Farmer in the Dell."

Jesus loves me so.
Yes, Jesus loves me so.
He is with me day and night,
He's with me wherever I go.

As you finish, tap a child on the head and ask him or her to follow you around the circle. Encourage the children to sing with you and continue until everyone is following you.

Keep singing the verse and begin to lead the group around the room. Add an action they can do while singing. For example, tap head, twirl slowly or clap hands above head. At the end of the verse, go to the back of the line and direct the child in front to lead with an action. Continue with the activity until everyone has had an opportunity to lead.

If a child hesitates to lead, invite him or her to come join you, and continue with the next person.

Conclude the activity by gathering in a circle, holding hands, singing the verse, and adding a jump and a "Hey!" at the end.

6. Door Hanger Design

(Photocopy the "Door Hanger" handout, one for each child. Photocopy them onto heavy paper or glue them on construction paper. Provide crayons, small pieces of different-color tissue paper and glue.)

Give each child a "Door Hanger" handout. Read the words on it: **"Jesus is with me!"** Let them decorate the hangers with crayons or by gluing crumpled tissue paper on them.

7. Jesus Hugs

(You'll need twisted pretzels, apple juice, napkins and cups.)

Serve pretzels and juice as the snack. Have children look at the pretzels and notice the cross pattern. Have them cross their arms in front of their chest in the same manner. Call this a "Jesus Hug." Say that even though we can't see Jesus, we can still feel his presence and pretend to feel his hugs.

With their arms crossed, lead them in this prayer: **Thank you, Jesus, for loving us and being with us wherever we go. Thank you for the food to make our bodies strong. Help us to feel your hugs every day. Amen.**

8. Picture Pass Around

(You'll need a picture of Jesus.)

Gather in a circle once more. Repeat Matthew 28:20: "I will be with you always." Show the children the picture of Jesus, then say: **Pictures of Jesus remind us that he is with us wherever we go.**

Pass the picture around the circle. As each child holds the picture, have him or her complete the sentence: "Jesus is with me when I _____."

Accept each answer even if it's repeated. Answers can be sleep, run, jump, talk, eat, cry.

When the picture returns to you, sum up all the responses as you lead children in the following reading. Fill in the blank with one of the kids' words and repeat until all the responses have been included.

Teacher: **For being with us when we** _____,

Children: Thank you, Jesus.

Encourage kids each to take home their door hanger. Ask them to hang it on their bedroom door knob as a reminder that Jesus is with them always.

by Jane P. Wilke

DOOR HANGER

TALKING TO GOD

Many young children love to pray, but they have lots of questions about how prayer works. They need to know that prayer is one way to talk to God. God hears our prayers and God answers our prayers.

Use this lesson to teach children more about prayer—a way to talk to God.

A POWERFUL PURPOSE

Preschool children will understand what prayer is and that God hears their prayers.

A LOOK AT THE LESSON

1. What Is Prayer? (up to 6 minutes)
2. God Answers Prayer
   (up to 6 minutes)
3. Fishy Snack (up to 6 minutes)
4. Prayer Topics (up to 6 minutes)
5. Prayer Necklaces
   (up to 6 minutes)
6. Pray Always (up to 3 minutes)
7. God Listens (up to 4 minutes)
8. Basket of Prayers
   (up to 3 minutes)
9. Thank You, God
   (up to 3 minutes)

A SPRINKLING OF SUPPLIES

Gather a Bible, photocopies of the handouts, a construction paper question mark, puppets, a table, a basket, fish-shape crackers, bread, butter, jelly, juice, cups, napkins, paper, crayons, a pen, scissors, posterboard, glue, a hole punch and yarn.

THE LIVELY LESSON

1. What Is Prayer?

(Use puppets to perform the "What Is Prayer?" skit. Turn a table on its side to use as a puppet stage. You'll also need a construction paper question mark.)

Welcome the children into the room and ask them to sit down. Introduce the two puppets and say: **Let's listen to these two people and see what we're going to learn today.**

When the puppets finish, have the children show their appreciation by giving them a standing ovation. Stand and clap and cheer!

2. God Answers Prayer

(You'll need a Bible, a basket, and cut-out fish and loaves from photocopies of the "Fish and Loaves" handout.)

Read about Jesus feeding a crowd of people in Matthew 14:13-21. Then tell children they're going to act out the story.

Ask one of the older children to be Jesus. Give this child a basket with the cut-out fish and loaves in the bottom. You'll need enough fish and loaves to distribute to each child and still have some left over. Don't allow the other children to see in the bottom of the basket.

WHAT IS PRAYER?

Actor 1: (Claps and jumps all around while looking up.)

Actor 2: (Enters) Hi. What are you doing?

Actor 1: (Keeps clapping.) Sh-h-h.

Actor 2: (Looks all around, confused. Then looks up.) Hey, what is it? Why are you clapping?

Actor 1: I'm not clapping.

Actor 2: Oh, yes, you are.

Actor 1: No, I'm not. I'm praying.

Actor 2: That's not praying. When you pray you bow your head and you have to be quiet.

Actor 1: Yeah. I do that some-times. But right now I'm just telling God how great I think he is. Why don't you join me? Yea, God!

Actor 2: (Joins and both say, "Yea, God!" and clap.)

Actor 2: (Bends over and picks up a question mark.) Wait a minute. Wait a minute.

Actor 1: Now what?

Actor 2: I want to ask God a question. Is that okay?

Actor 1: Sure it is. That's part of prayer too.

Actor 2: You mean if we don't understand something, we can ask God about it in prayer?

Actor 1: Sure! God wants us to ask questions. So go ahead.

Actor 2: (Bows head, then looks up.) Okay, I'm doing it.

Actor 1: Well, what'd you ask?

Actor 2: I asked God to teach me more about prayer because I like talking to him.

Choose two or three others to be disciples. Give them five loaves of bread and two fish.

Everyone else plays the hungry crowd.

Narrate the story and help children act out their parts.

Jesus saw a huge crowd of people and felt sorry for them. (Jesus looks around at the crowd of people.)

It was late in the day and they were hungry. (Kids rub their tummies and moan, "We're hungry.")

The disciples came to Jesus. (Walk toward Jesus.)

They said: "We can't feed them. We only have five loaves of bread and two fish." (Show the five loaves and two fish to Jesus.)

Jesus said, "Give them to me." (Disciples give them to Jesus.)

He took them, (Take them.)

Looked up to heaven, (Look up.)

Prayed over them, (Hold up the loaves and fish.)

Put them in a basket, (Put them in your basket.)

And said, "Give them to the people." (Jesus says, "Give them to the people.")

The disciples gave out the food. (Disciples take Jesus' basket and give out the food to each person in the crowd.)

The people ate until they were full. (Pretend to eat the fish and loaves, then lean back and groan, "Oh, we're full.")

Everyone was amazed because there were 12 baskets of food left over. (Everyone says, "Wow!")

After the story, have kids give themselves a standing ovation. Stand and clap and cheer!

Afterward say: **When we pray, God hears our prayers and answers them. We're going to learn more about prayer today.**

3. Fishy Snack

(You'll need fish-shape crackers, bread, butter, jelly, juice, cups and napkins.)

Tell children they're going to eat some food like the people did in the Bible story. Serve fish-shape crackers and bread with butter and jelly. Kids can drink juice. Pray before the snack, asking God to bless the food.

4. Prayer Topics

(You'll need photocopies of the "Prayer Topics" handout and crayons.)

When kids finish their snack, give them each a "Prayer Topic" handout and some crayons. Explain the things we pray about shown on the handout: when we get hurt, when we're afraid, our family, someone who is sick, food.

Say: **Color the pictures. Think about each thing as you color its picture. What else do you pray about? Draw those things in the blank squares. Maybe you have a problem with a friend or you're worried about your parents. God wants us to pray about all of our concerns.**

5. Prayer Necklaces

(You'll need scissors, posterboard squares the same size as each square on the "Prayer Topics" handout, glue, a hole punch and 20-inch pieces of yarn.)

Encourage children each to choose one thing they'd like to pray about today. Have them cut that picture from their "Prayer Topic" handout and glue it to a posterboard square. You may need to help younger preschoolers

FISH AND LOAVES

PRAYER TOPICS

PRAYER TOPICS

with cutting out the pictures.

Assist the children in punching a hole in each square and threading a 20-inch piece of yarn through the hole. Hang the prayer necklace around the child's neck. Make a necklace for yourself also.

6. Pray Always

Ask kids to gather in a circle. Help them memorize this paraphrase of 1 Thessalonians 5:16-18. You say a phrase and show an action. Then have children repeat what you say and do.

Be happy. (Smile.)

Pray always. (Fold hands, bow heads.)

Thank God for everything. (Hold both hands up, look up to heaven.)

After kids memorize the words and actions, do the actions and ask kids to supply the words.

Finally, have everyone do a silent version of the memorized verse. Have everyone do the actions only—no words.

7. God Listens

(You'll need slips of paper and a pen.)

Have children sit on the floor in front of you. Show them your necklace and tell them what you want to pray about. Write your prayer request on a slip of paper.

Tell children they can pray to God and that he always listens. God wants us to tell him any problem or any concern we have. He'll answer our prayer.

One at a time, ask children each to show their necklace and tell what they want to pray for. Write each request on a slip of paper, then hand the slip to the child.

After each child receives his or her slip, all children say, "God listens when we pray" and pat their knees for each syllable.

8. Basket of Prayers

(You'll need the slips of prayer requests and the basket you used in the "God Answers Prayer" activity.)

Tell children: **You're each holding a slip of paper that tells your prayer request. One at a time, stand up, come to me and put your prayer request in this basket.**

After your basket is full, invite kids to pray silently for these requests. Have kids bow their heads and fold their hands.

Hold up the basket and say: **Dear God. Thank you for hearing our prayers. We trust you to answer them. Amen.**

9. Thank You, God

Remind kids that their memory verse said to pray always and thank God for everything.

One at a time have kids say one thing they're thankful for. After each child says an item, have all kids clap and shout, "Thank you, God." Let every person contribute, with the whole group shouting, "Thank you, God" after each contribution.

by Christine Yount

GOD'S GIFT— FORGIVENESS

We all feel guilty at times and are hard on ourselves. We wish we would've done things differently. We kick ourselves for saying something mean or selfish.

Preschoolers are not immune to guilt. They may feel sorry when they do something wrong, hurt their brothers or sisters, or hit their friends. Some innocent children feel guilty when their parents divorce.

Use this lesson to talk about the forgiveness Jesus offers.

A POWERFUL PURPOSE

Preschool children will learn that Jesus forgives us and wants us to forgive others.

A LOOK AT THE LESSON

1. Which Way Do I Go? (up to 6 minutes)
2. A Bible Story (up to 4 minutes)
3. Banquet Time (up to 6 minutes)
4. We Are All Forgiven (up to 4 minutes)
5. How Do You Feel? (up to 4 minutes)
6. Forgive Others (up to 4 minutes)
7. Memory Tune (up to 6 minutes)
8. Musical Chairs (up to 6 minutes)

A SPRINKLING OF SUPPLIES

Gather a Bible, masking tape, paper, a marker, colorful stickers, paper plates, napkins, cups, juice, grapes, cheese and crackers, photocopies of the handout, crayons, chairs, a tape of lively music and a tape player.

THE LIVELY LESSON

1. Which Way Do I Go?

(Use masking tape to lay out two different "roads" as shown in the "Roads" diagram. Begin at your room's entrance and end up on the other side. Put a happy face on the wall at the end of one road and a sad face at the end of the other road.)

ROADS

Greet each child and tell him or her to choose one of the roads and follow it to the end. Say: **If you find a happy face at the end of your road, sit down below the sign, if you find a sad face go back and follow the other road.**

When everyone is sitting under the happy face, give kids each a bright-color sticker. Say: **Sometimes we do bad things. That's like going down the wrong road. But if we do something bad, God will forgive us if we** ask him to. Then we can continue on a good road by doing what's right. God's forgiveness makes us happy.

2. A Bible Story

(You'll need a Bible.)

Say: **Here's a Bible story about a son who took the wrong road and did the wrong thing. When the son felt bad for what he did, he told his father, "I'm sorry." His dad said: "It's okay. I love you." His dad forgave him.**

Read from a children's Bible the story of the prodigal son in Luke 15:11-24.

Say: **God is like the father in the story who forgave his son. When the son admitted he'd sinned, the father forgave him. God always forgives us when we ask for his forgiveness, and he wants us to forgive others who do bad things to us.**

Have children stand. Tell kids you're going to read some questions. If their answer is "Happy," they should jump up and down and say "Happy." If their answer is "Sad," they should slowly sit down and say "Sad."

Practice a couple times. Then read these questions:

● **At the end of the story, how do you think the dad felt when his boy returned home?**

● **At the beginning of the story, how do you think the dad felt about his son leaving?**

● **How do you think the younger son felt when he returned home and his dad welcomed him and forgave him?**

● **How do you feel when someone forgives you and says, "It's okay"?**

3. Banquet Time

(Prepare a table with paper plates, napkins, cups, juice, grapes, and cheese and crackers.)

Ask one more question: **How do you feel knowing we're going to eat snacks and celebrate God's forgiveness?**

Since almost everyone should be jumping up and down and saying, "Happy," tell them they look like they would enjoy a forgiveness banquet—like the man gave his son in the story.

Lead them to the table and sit down for a meal. Pass out paper plates, napkins and cups.

Pass around the grapes and say: **Eat some grapes. Celebrate God's gift of forgiveness.**

Pass around the cheese and crackers and say: **Eat some cheese and crackers. Fill up. God blesses us so much we overflow with his goodness.**

Fill each cup with juice and say: **Drink this juice and remember that all good things—especially forgiveness—come from God.**

4. We Are All Forgiven

Play a post-banquet party game. Teach kids these words to the tune of "One Little, Two Little, Three Little Indians."

**God forgives his little children,
God forgives his little children,
God forgives his little children,
When they seek forgiveness.**

Gather in a circle and sing the song as you march clockwise. The second time you sing, have kids each find a partner, face each other, grab hands and go sideways around the circle counterclockwise. The third time you sing, have everyone march clockwise again.

5. How Do You Feel?

(You'll need photocopies of the "How Do You Feel?" handout and crayons.)

Sit down in the circle after you finish the song. Give kids each a "How Do You Feel?" handout and crayons. Tell them to hold the handout so the face looks happy. Next, have them turn the handout upside down. The face now looks sad. Give children a couple of minutes to color the face.

Say: **I'm going to ask you a few questions. If the answer is "happy," hold up the happy face. If it's "sad," turn the paper so the frowning face shows.**

Ask:

● **How do you feel after our banquet?**

● **How do you feel when someone hurts you?**

● **How do you feel when you forgive that person and say, "It's okay"?**

● **How would you feel if I said, "It's time to say goodbye"?**

● **How would you feel if I said, "We still have more fun activities to do, we won't say goodbye for a while"?**

6. Forgive Others

(Each child will need the "How Do You Feel?" handout.)

Say: **When God forgives us we feel good. Others feel good when we forgive them. I'll read some stories, and you answer my questions by turning your paper to a smile or a frown, depending on your answer.**

● **Tiffany was playing with Tom's toy lawnmower and broke off one of its wheels. How does Tiffany feel? How does Tom feel?**

● **Tom got angry at Tiffany and made her go away. How does Tiffany feel? How does Tom feel?**

● **Tom said he would forgive Tiffany and gave Tiffany another toy to play with. How does Tiffany feel? How does Tom feel? How does God feel?**

● **Jeff, Chris and Terry are playing together in the yard. How do they feel?**

● **Jeff and Chris ignore Terry and won't let her play with them. How does Terry feel?**

● **Terry gets mad and starts yelling. How does Terry feel?**

● **Jeff and Chris say they're sorry and Terry forgives them. They keep playing. How does Terry feel? How does God feel? How do Jeff and Chris feel?**

7. Memory Tune

(You'll need a tape of lively music and a tape player.)

Let kids learn this Bible verse in a fun way: "Forgive each other" (Ephesians 4:32). Play lively music and ask kids to move around the room—hop, skip, walk, march, any movement they want. When you stop the music, have children each hug a person standing close to them and say, "Forgive each other." Start the music again and continue until kids have each hugged several different people and repeated the verse several times.

8. Musical Chairs

(You'll need chairs set up in a circle, enough for every child except one.)

Play a game of musical chairs, only don't eliminate anyone. Have children march around the chairs and sing the following song with you. When you stop singing, they should all sit down. One child will be without a seat. He or she should begin the song to start kids marching again. Sing the song to the tune of "Row, Row, Row Your Boat."

Sin, sin, sin is bad,
But our Lord forgives.
Aren't we really, really glad?
Yes, our Lord forgives.
                    by Ray and Cindy Peppers

HOW DO YOU FEEL?

HEAVEN: HOME, SWEET HOME

It is hard for a child to get a clear and reassuring picture of our eternal home. Simplify this concept by comparing heaven to the very best earthly home.

Use this lesson to show kids that though we don't know everything about heaven, we do know one important fact: Heaven will one day be our home, where we'll live with our heavenly father and the wonderful family he has given us to love.

A POWERFUL PURPOSE

Preschool children will learn that heaven is a place they'll like.

A LOOK AT THE LESSON

1. Squirrel at Home
   (up to 6 minutes)
2. In a Sack (up to 3 minutes)
3. Seeing Is Believing
   (up to 4 minutes)
4. Pictures of Home
   (up to 6 minutes)
5. What Makes a Home?
   (up to 4 minutes)
6. Heaven: Home, Sweet Home
   (up to 6 minutes)
7. What Is Heaven?
   (up to 6 minutes)
8. Heavenly Honey Biscuits
   (up to 6 minutes)

A SPRINKLING OF SUPPLIES

Gather a Bible, a doll in a sack, large pieces of construction paper, crayons, photocopies of the handout, biscuits, butter, honey in squeeze bottles, juice, cups, napkins and supplies to clean hands.

THE LIVELY LESSON

1. Squirrel at Home

Welcome the children and play a fun game to get them ready to learn. Choose one child to be an extra squirrel, then form teams of three with the rest of the kids. Have two members of each team make a "hollow tree" by standing facing each other, with their hands on each other's shoulders. Have the third team member play a "squirrel" by standing between the other two, at home in the tree. When you clap your hands, each squirrel must find a new home tree. The extra squirrel tries to find a home too. Whichever child is left out at the end of the run is the extra squirrel for the next time.

Play a few times, then switch so the "hollow trees" can be squirrels too. Rotate in any players who didn't get to play the first round.

Say: **You all played squirrels at home in their trees. Our homes are in houses, apartments or buildings. But today we're going to talk about heaven—our home when we go to live with Jesus forever.**

2. In a Sack

(You'll need a doll in a sack.)
Hold up the sack with the doll

inside. Ask the children to describe the doll you're holding up. They may be able to guess that it has arms and legs and a face, but since they can't see it, they won't be able to describe it in detail.

Take the doll out of the bag. Hold it up so everyone can see it, then say: **Now tell me what the doll looks like.**

They'll tell you all they can see: hair color, eye color, what it's wearing.

3. Seeing Is Believing

Pass around the doll while you discuss these questions:

● **Why couldn't you describe the doll when it was in a sack?**

● **Were there things you could guess about the doll even when you couldn't see it?**

Say: **It's hard to describe something you can't see. That's just like heaven. It's hard to describe because we haven't seen it yet.**

4. Pictures of Home

(You'll need crayons and large pieces of construction paper. Lay them on the floor.)

Have kids follow you to the construction paper and crayons. As they follow you, march to the chant:

**Heaven is a wonderful place;
It will be our home someday.**

Have children each find a piece of paper to draw on. Tell them to draw a picture of their home. When everyone is finished, take a walking tour around the pictures. As you walk and look, say the chant again.

5. What Makes a Home?

Let each child discuss his or her picture.

Adapt the following discussion depending on the children in your group. Be sensitive to kids whose homes might not be happy—through death or divorce. Emphasize that heaven will be better than even the best earthly home.

Say: **Our homes are special places. Most of us like our homes very much, and we wouldn't feel at home in any other house. Why is that? Is it because of the walls? the rooms? the windows? the furniture? All of our homes probably have these things. So there's nothing really special about them, is there? What does your home have that no other home has?**

Let kids try to guess, then say: **The people who live in our homes make our homes special.**

6. Heaven: Home, Sweet Home

(You'll need crayons and photocopies of the "Heaven: Home, Sweet Home" handout. Lay the handouts and crayons on the floor.)

Ask kids to follow behind you to another area of the room where you've laid the handouts and crayons. As they follow, march to the same chant:

**Heaven is a wonderful place;
It will be our home someday.**

Read the handouts to the kids: "Heaven: Home, Sweet Home." Have them draw a picture of heaven as they imagine it—pretty clouds, warm sunshine, happy people.

After they finish, walk around their drawings as you say the chant again.

7. What Is Heaven?

(You'll need a Bible.)

Say: **Heaven is God's home. Jesus lives there and someday we will**

too. Listen as I read what Jesus says.

Read John 14:3: "After I go and prepare a place for you, I will come back. Then I will take you to be with me so that you may be where I am."

Say: **You drew your ideas of heaven. Lots of people wonder what heaven will look like. But no one but God knows for sure. We haven't ever seen it. Remember how you couldn't describe the doll because you couldn't see it? Well, heaven is hard to describe too. But the Bible tells us about heaven.**

Read the following descriptions and direct kids to respond after each description.

● **Matthew 6:20 says we will have treasures in heaven.** (Have kids say, "O-o-o-o-o-o-o.")

● **John 14:2 says there are many rooms there for lots of people.** (Have kids spread their arms wide.)

● **Revelation 19:1 says that those who live in heaven will shout praises to God.** (Have everyone shout, "I love you God!")

● **Revelation 21:3-4 says God will live with us there and will wipe all our tears away. There won't be any more crying or death or sadness.** (Have everyone smile big smiles.)

So heaven will one day be the home where God lives with all of us, his children. (Have everyone link arms in a circle and sit down.)

8. Heavenly Honey Biscuits

(You'll need biscuits, butter, honey in squeeze bottles, juice, cups, napkins and supplies to clean hands.)

Serve biscuits, butter, honey and juice. Then pray: **Thank you, God, that you're making a wonderful home for us in heaven. Thank you for loving us so much that you want to live there with us forever. Amen.**

Sing songs such as "Heaven Is a Wonderful Place" and "Do, Lord."

Let kids take home their two drawings—their earthly home and their heavenly home.

by Karen M. Ball

HEAVEN: HOME, SWEET HOME

PART 4:
A LIVELY LOOK
at CELEBRATIONS

A BIRTHDAY BONANZA

Preschool children are learning about themselves, especially about what they can do. They're in a concrete stage of learning and don't understand symbolism. Each new learning experience (especially when presented in an active, fun way) provides important information about their capabilities and enhances self-esteem.

Use this lesson to show kids how much they're growing and how they're learning new things.

A POWERFUL PURPOSE

Preschool children will celebrate their birthdays and see that the bigger they grow the more they know.

A LOOK AT THE LESSON

1. Babies Can't Do This
   (up to 3 minutes)
2. My Hand Prints: I Am Growing
   (up to 6 minutes)
3. Birthday Balloons: Getting Bigger and Bigger (up to 3 minutes)
4. Happy Birthday to Me
   (up to 5 minutes)
5. Birthday Party Snack
   (up to 6 minutes)
6. Jesus Grew Too (up to 3 minutes)
7. I'm Not a Baby, I'm Not a Grownup (up to 6 minutes)
8. See How Tall I Grow to Be
   (up to 6 minutes)
9. Thanks for Birthdays and Growing (up to 2 minutes)

A SPRINKLING OF SUPPLIES

Gather a Bible, a baby-size doll, bright-color tempera paint, flat pans, old shirts or aprons, colored construction paper, photocopies of the handout, glue, balloons and frosted cupcakes. For each child, you'll need one item of baby or adult clothing.

THE LIVELY LESSON

1. Babies Can't Do This

As children arrive, seat them in a circle. Ask them, one by one: **What can you do that a baby can't do? Show me!** For example, they can run, jump, talk, hop or sing.

After each child shows you something, say: **When you were a baby, you couldn't do these things, but now you can, because you're growing.**

2. My Hand Prints: I Am Growing

(You'll need the baby-size doll, bright-color tempera paint in flat pans, photocopies of the "My Hand Prints" handout, old shirts or aprons. Ask someone to help you with this activity.)

Pass around the doll and ask the children each to hold their hand up to the doll's hand. Say: **Something else that tells us we're growing is that we get bigger. Look at your hands and see how much bigger they are than the doll's hands. Are your**

hands bigger than a baby's hands?

Tell them they're going to make prints of their hands, which are bigger than a baby's but still smaller than a grownup's.

Hold up a "My Hand Prints" handout and read the poem.

> **Here are hand prints of me**
> **Made for people to see.**
> **Though to you I seem small,**
> **God will help me grow tall**

Cover the kids' good clothes with the old shirts or aprons. Dip the palms of their hands in the tempera paint and press them firmly on their handout. Have someone help the children wash their hands afterward. Write each child's name on his or her paper.

3. Birthday Balloons: Getting Bigger and Bigger

(You'll need an inflated balloon for each person.)

Say: **We use balloons to celebrate birthdays. But did you know that a balloon can grow like your body grows?**

Show kids a deflated balloon, then say: **See how small this balloon is? Watch what happens to it.**

Blow into the balloon 'til it's one-fourth full. Say: **This balloon is like a 1-year-old.** Add a bit more air and say: **Now it's like a 2-year-old.** And so on, until the balloon is "like a 5-year-old." Say: **This balloon grew just as you are growing. I'm going to give you each a balloon. We're going to bat the balloons in the air.**

Pass out one inflated balloon to each child and allow a couple minutes of "balloon-batting." The goal is that the balloons stay in the air. As kids bat balloons, lead them in saying "Growing, growing, we are growing."

After balloons have been batted for a while, gather them and let kids take them home after the lesson.

4. Happy Birthday to Me

Gather in a circle again. Say: **One thing that happens when we grow is that we have birthdays!** Announce that you're going to celebrate everyone's birthday today and need help singing "Happy Birthday" in a new way. Have them sing:

> **Happy birthday to me,**
> **Happy birthday to me,**
> **Happy birthday, dear** (All children shout out their own name.),
> **Happy birthday to me!**

If you have time, you could sing through the song once for every child.

5. Birthday Party Snack

(You'll need frosted cupcakes, one for each child.)

Pass out the frosted cupcakes as you say: **Happy birthday, birthday kids. Have some birthday cake.**

6. Jesus Grew Too

(You'll need a Bible.)

While kids are eating, say: **Did you know that Jesus was once a child too? We celebrate his birthday at Christmas. After Jesus was a baby, he grew to be your age. Listen to what the Bible tells us.**

Read Luke 2:52 from a children's Bible, or use this version: "Jesus continued to learn more and more and to grow physically. People liked him, and he pleased God."

Say: **Jesus grew up as a chld just like you're growing up.**

After kids swallow the last of their cupcakes, say: **Let's sing Jesus a birthday song too.** Sing these words:

> **Happy birthday to you,**

MY HAND PRINTS

Here are hand prints of me
Made for people to see.
Though to you I seem small,
God will help me grow tall!

Happy birthday to you,
Happy birthday, dear Jesus,
We sure do love you!

7. I'm Not a Baby, I'm Not a Grownup

(Place the baby and adult clothes in the center of the room.)

Gather children in a circle around the clothes. One at a time have children each pick out one item of clothing and take it back to their seat.

After everyone has done this, go around the circle and invite kids to try on their chosen items. Ask children questions such as: **What's wrong with that item? How does it feel? Is it too big or too small?**

With each item of baby clothing, say something like: **Those baby clothes are too small for you.** With each item of adult clothing say something like: **Those grown-up clothes are too big for you.**

After everyone has had a turn, say: **As you can see, you're no longer babies, but you're not yet grown-ups. You are you. Right now. Each of you is a special person. You're growing bigger each day, and you'll keep growing. Each inch you grow, each day of your life, you learn new things. That's the way God made you.**

8. See How Tall I Grow to Be

Sing this action song to the tune of "Twinkle, Twinkle, Little Star." Have children repeat each line with actions, then slowly combine all lines together.

See how tall I grow to be. (Stretch hands above head.)
Inch by inch I grow, you see. (Stretch hands above head "inch by inch" with each word.)
I'm not a baby any more. (Rock baby.)
Soon I'll even go to school. (Skip.)
See how tall I grow to be. (Stretch on toes.)
God made you, (Point to others.)
And God made me. (Point to self.)

9. Thanks for Birthdays and Growing

Ask children to hold hands in a circle and bow their heads. Pray: **Thank you, God, for making me and for giving me a family who loves me. Thank you for each birthday and that I am growing each day. Amen.**

Give kids their balloons to take home. As you hand out the balloons say: **Happy Birthday!**

by Jerayne Gray-Reneberg

THE REASON FOR EASTER

Easter can mean a lot of things to young children: Easter egg hunts, baskets and bunnies. Easter can also mean a time of big meals, family gatherings, church services and songs.

Use this lesson to help children talk about Easter. Help them focus on the real reason for Easter—Jesus.

A POWERFUL PURPOSE

Preschool children will learn more about Jesus and about Easter.

A LOOK AT THE LESSON

1. Class Crier (Interspersed throughout the meeting)
2. Jesus Died for My Sins (up to 4 minutes)
3. Resurrection Buns (up to 6 minutes)
4. The Easter Story (up to 5 minutes)
5. Eyewitness Report (up to 6 minutes)
6. Up, Up, Up (up to 4 minutes)
7. Easter Baskets (up to 5 minutes)
8. Easter Cross Hunt (up to 6 minutes)
9. Prayer Time (up to 4 minutes)

A SPRINKLING OF SUPPLIES

Gather a Bible or a book for children that tells the Easter story, yellow posterboard, robe, two Resurrection Buns per child, sandwich bags, photocopies of the handouts, three puppets made from socks or sacks, cardboard, a marker, tape, stapler and staples, a table, Easter stickers, yarn, construction paper, sequins, glue, scissors, and one plastic gallon milk jug per child.

THE LIVELY LESSON

1. Class Crier

(Ask an adult or teenager to perform as the class crier four times during the lesson. Read the lesson ahead of time to see when the class crier walks through. The first three times, the crier holds up a yellow sun cut from posterboard. The crier moves the sun in an overhead arc as though the sun has risen and set on another day. The person should wear a robe and dress like a follower of Jesus.)

When children have arrived, have the class crier give the first cry: "Oh, my. Jesus is dead. He died on a cross."

Welcome the kids and say: **That was our class crier who'll tell us Easter messages throughout our time together.**

2. Jesus Died for My Sins

Ask kids to join hands in a circle and walk clockwise as they sing this song to the tune of "London Bridge."
**Jesus died for my sins,
For my sins,
For my sins;
Jesus died for my sins,
I'm forgiven.**
Have kids sing the song several times, then sit down in a circle. Say: **We're going to talk about Easter—**

about Jesus dying for our sins and rising from the dead. When Jesus died on a cross, he was buried in a tomb, which is a cave for people who have died.

Have the class crier cry a second time: "Oh, no. Jesus is buried in a tomb."

Say: **But that's not the end of the story.**

3. Resurrection Buns

(You'll need Resurrection Buns made according to the recipe on the handout.)

Give each child a Resurrection Bun. As kids bite into their buns, they'll discover the buns' hollow insides contain a sugary surprise.

Say: **You're surprised at the inside of your Resurrection Bun. The disciples were also surprised on the first Easter. They went inside the tomb where Jesus was buried and discovered something. It was empty.**

Have the class crier give the third cry: "I'm so sad that Jesus is dead."

4. The Easter Story

(You'll need a children's Bible or a book that tells the Easter story for children.)

Read the Easter story from John 20:1-8 or from a children's book.

Ask kids to close their eyes and picture the story in their minds. Imagine . . .

  . . . early morning
  . . . going to the tomb
  . . . seeing the big rock used to cover the opening was rolled away
  . . . Mary running to tell the others
  . . . Peter and the other disciple running back to the tomb

  . . . seeing the tomb was empty
  . . . Jesus was not there

Have the class crier cry out the fourth time: "He's alive! He's alive! He's alive!"

5. Eyewitness Report

(You'll need the "Eyewitness Report" skit and three puppets—a reporter and two disciples. Make simple puppets out of socks or sacks. Use a marker to design faces. Tape a cardboard microphone to the front of the reporter puppet. Ask three adults or three teenagers to perform this puppet skit. Turn a table on its side and use it for a stage.)

Have everyone follow the class crier around the room. Everyone marches behind the crier chanting: "He's alive! He's alive! He's alive!" The class crier leads them over to the puppet stage.

When kids are seated, begin the "Eyewitness Report" puppet show.

6. Up, Up, Up

After the puppet show, say: **We're going to celebrate that surprising report that Jesus is alive. He rose from the dead.**

Teach children this Easter action song to the tune of "Row, Row, Row Your Boat." Repeat the song and actions several times.

  Up, (Touch the floor.)
  Up, (Touch your thighs.)
  Up (Touch your shoulders.)
  He rose; (Wave hands above head.)
  Jesus is alive. (Clap, clap, clap.)
  Jesus is alive today. (Wave hands above head.)
  Jesus is alive. (Clap, clap, clap.)

7. Easter Baskets

(For each child, you'll need an empty plastic gallon milk jug. You'll also need a stapler, Easter stickers, yarn,

RESURRECTION BUNS

Frozen bread dough

Butter

24 marshmallows

1 cup sugar

2 teaspoons cinnamon

Let the frozen dough thaw.

Melt some butter.

In a separate bowl, mix the sugar and cinnamon together.

Divide dough into 24 uniform balls. Roll each ball out until flat. Wrap each flattened ball around a marshmallow, making sure to seal all openings. Dip the ball in melted butter, then in the sugar and cinnamon mixture.

Place in a large, greased baking pan. Cover and let rise until double (about 35 minutes). Bake at 375° for 18 to 20 minutes. Makes 24.

EYEWITNESS REPORT

The reporter puppet stands on the stage. Two disciple puppets run across the stage and almost knock the reporter over.

Reporter: Hey, what's going on here?

Disciple 1: Haven't you heard the news?

Disciple 2: I thought everyone knew by now!

Reporter: What news? Knew what? (Points microphone toward each puppet's face as he talks.)

Disciple 1: He's alive!

Disciple 2: He has risen!

Reporter: What? Are you saying a dead person is now alive?

Both: Yes! Jesus is alive! (Reporter is confused about where to point the microphone.)

Reporter: Jesus? Who is this Jesus?

Disciple 1: He is the Son of God.

Reporter: And you say he died. How did this Jesus die?

Disciple 2: It was three days ago. The saddest day of our lives.

Disciple 1: They hung Jesus on a cross and killed him.

Reporter: What did he do wrong?

Disciple 1: Nothing. They just wanted to kill him.

Disciple 2: And he died. And we thought it was all over.

Disciple 1: But today we saw him! We saw his hands and feet where the nails had been.

Disciple 2: And he ate with us.

Reporter: A dead man is alive? How?

Disciple 1: God raised him from the dead.

Reporter: Why did God raise Jesus from the dead?

Disciple 2: So we can live forever, just like Jesus!

Reporter: What?

Disciple 1: Don't you see? Jesus is God's gift to us. If we accept God's gift of Jesus, we'll live forever too.

Reporter: (Turns to audience.) Well, you heard it, folks. Jesus was killed and buried in a tomb for three days. But now he's alive. This is Perry Puppet reporting live from Jerusalem on Easter morning.

construction paper, sequins and glue. Cut the gallon jugs in half. Cut a 1-inch ring from the bottom of the upper half of the jug. Clip the ring to make a strip of plastic. Staple this strip to the bottom half of the jug to make a handle for the basket as shown in the "Basket" diagram.)

Say: **Let's make Easter baskets from the supplies. Decorate them any way you want.**

You make one too so kids can see an example.

BASKET

HANDLE

BASKET

8. Easter Cross Hunt

(For each child, you'll need 10 construction paper crosses.)

While kids finish decorating their baskets, hide the crosses in the room.

Say: **Since Jesus is the real reason for Easter, we're not going to look for Easter eggs today; we're going to look for Easter crosses. We're celebrating because Jesus died on a cross and lives again.**

Let kids hunt for the Easter crosses and put them in their baskets.

9. Prayer Time

(For each child, you'll need a photocopy of the "Resurrection Buns" handout and a Resurrection Bun in a sandwich bag.)

After the hunt, gather the children. Instead of forming a circle, form a cross. Pray: **Thank you, Jesus, for dying for us on a cross and for rising from the dead on Easter. Amen.**

Give kids each a photocopy of the "Resurrection Bun" handout and put a wrapped Resurrection Bun in each child's basket. Let kids take their baskets home and have a wonderful Easter.

by Christine Yount

A THANKFUL THANKSGIVING

Young children are interested in doing things with their friends. They also love to hear stories—especially stories that happened long ago or "Once upon a time . . ."

Use this lesson to help preschoolers learn about Thanksgiving. Give them an opportunity to thank God for blessings in their lives.

A POWERFUL PURPOSE

Preschool children will give thanks, as the pilgrims did, for blessings in their lives.

A LOOK AT THE LESSON

1. God Loves Me Every Day
   (up to 5 minutes)
2. Shake a Story (up to 6 minutes)
3. Pat a Pilgrims' Prayer
   (up to 3 minutes)
4. Friendship Feast
   (up to 6 minutes)
5. Seeds Are Beautiful
   (up to 6 minutes)
6. We Give Thanks
   (up to 6 minutes)
7. Great Growth Charts
   (up to 6 minutes)
8. God's Love Keeps Growing
   (up to 2 minutes)

A SPRINKLING OF SUPPLIES

Gather one pint of heavy whipping cream, one see-through plastic container with a tight-fitting lid, crackers, knife, salt, yellow food coloring (op-

tional), a small bowl, chocolate milk, different types of seeds (pumpkin, sunflower, sesame, apple), different-color construction paper, glue, a tape measure, butcher paper, a marker, crayons, straight pins and a bulletin board.

THE LIVELY LESSON

1. God Loves Me Every Day

Greet the children then gather in a circle. Tell them they're going to learn about Thanksgiving and have a chance to give thanks for their blessings.

Teach children this song to the tune of "Twinkle, Twinkle Little Star." Have them repeat, line by line with actions, then slowly combine all lines together.

I know God loves me every day. (Hug self.)

God shows me in many ways: (Arms extended, separated lightly, palms up.)

My family and my friends he gave, (Hands over heart.)

And the good food that I eat. (Touch lips.)

God's good blessings with me stay. (Arms raised, palms open.)

I know God loves me every day. (Hug self.)

2. Shake a Story

(Pour the heavy whipping cream into the see-through container with a tight-fitting lid. Shake the container for five to six minutes to begin the butter-making process. Kids will continue to shake during the activity—approximately 2 to 3 more minutes.)

Pass around the container filled with heavy whipping cream. Explain that the kids will take turns shaking the container to make butter while you tell the story of the Pilgrims.

Once upon a time, long ago, the Pilgrims came to America. These people came from across the sea. When they got here, though, they didn't know how to grow foods in a new land. So the Indians showed them how to grow things like corn, pumpkins and beans and how to prepare and eat turkey. Without the Indians' help, the Pilgrims would have had little to eat and would have starved.

The first year, when all the foods were ready to eat, the Pilgrims had a big feast and invited their Indian friends. They thanked God for all the delicious new foods and for their new friends. And each Thanksgiving Day we do the same thing when we thank God for food, friends, families and all the gifts God gives us.

Say: **Today we'll celebrate our own Friendship Feast with the butter you've just been making. Let's thank God for our butter and all our blessings.**

3. Pat a Pilgrim's Prayer

Ask kids to pat their knees in rhythm. Tell them they're going to pat a prayer to a one-two beat. Ask the kids to repeat each line after you say it. Keep the patting rhythm going throughout the prayer.

Thank you, God,
For these gifts:

Food,
Families,
Friends,
Our beautiful earth,
Us,
Jesus.
He sure loves us.
He calls us friends.
Amen!

4. Friendship Feast

(You'll need a Bible, the butter, crackers, salt, yellow food coloring, a bowl and a butter knife.)

Help the children remove the lid from the container. Pour off the liquid into the empty bowl. Add salt to taste and yellow food coloring. Spread on crackers. Also serve chocolate milk or another drink kids will be thankful for.

Say: **There's a Bible verse that's nice for Thanksgiving. Listen to it as you eat your crackers and butter.**

Read Psalm 107:1 from a children's Bible, or use this version: "Thank the Lord because he is good. His love continues forever!"

5. Seeds Are Beautiful

(You'll need construction paper, glue and seeds.)

Tell kids they're going to make seed pictures by gluing seeds onto construction paper. Older kids may want to glue seeds in the shape of the Earth, their friends, their families, their pets, their churches, their homes, or whatever they're thankful for. Others may want to create a free design. Let the children glue seeds on their paper in any way they choose.

Say: **Seeds are one thing to thank God for. We can use them for food or plant them to grow more food.**

6. We Give Thanks

(You'll need straight pins and a bulletin board titled "We Give Thanks.")

Gather in a circle. Ask the children each to show their picture and explain what they're thankful for. Pin the pictures to the bulletin board titled "We Give Thanks." Read the bulletin board title to the kids.

7. Great Growth Charts

(Make growth charts by cutting 6-inch-by-2-feet butcher paper strips, one for each child. With a marker, mark 1-inch measurements along the side. Start at the bottom with 24 inches and go up to 48 inches. You'll also need crayons.)

Say: **Food is not the only thing that grows. What else grows that we're thankful for?**

Say: **There are lots of things that grow. Even you! Now we're going to make a growth chart so you can measure how much you grow.**

Give each child a growth chart prepared earlier. Let kids each decorate their chart to take home and hang on the wall.

Help them measure their present height. Tell kids to thank God for his measureless, endless love each time they measure their growth.

8. God's Love Keeps Growing

(You'll need the completed growth charts.)

Ask children to bring their competed growth charts and gather in a circle. For a closing prayer, begin with: **Thanks, God, for your love that keeps growing . . .** Have kids, one at a time, say "and growing" as they hold up their growth chart. Continue around the circle so each child has a chance to add to the prayer. When it gets back to you, say: **Amen!**

by Jerayne Gray-Reneberg

CHRISTMAS CELEBRATION

Babies, babies everywhere. All of us were once babies. The Christmas story tells of Jesus' birth and the miraculous events surrounding the beginning of this special baby's life.

Use this lesson to show similarities and differences between babies now and the baby Jesus on the first Christmas.

A POWERFUL PURPOSE

Preschool children will relate their own experiences with babies to the baby Jesus of long ago.

A LOOK AT THE LESSON

1. Baby Hide-and-Seek
   (up to 5 minutes)
2. What Do You Know About
   Babies? (up to 3 minutes)
3. Action-Packed Story
   (up to 4 minutes)
4. Snackin' Time (up to 3 minutes)
5. Jesus' Birthday (up to 3 minutes)
6. Wrapping Baby Jesus
   (up to 6 minutes)
7. Rattle Rhymes (up to 4 minutes)
8. Christmas Sing-Along
   (up to 5 minutes)
9. Christmas Prayer
   (up to 2 minutes)

A SPRINKLING OF SUPPLIES

Gather a diaper, diaper pin, baby powder, ointment, booties, receiving blanket, spoons, napkins, a Bible, photocopies of the handout, scrap fabric cut in strips, crayons, glue, pots, pans, lids, bowls, baby-food jars. For each child, you'll also need applesauce and a baby rattle.

THE LIVELY LESSON

1. Baby Hide-and-Seek

(On a table place a diaper, diaper pin, baby powder, ointment, booties and one receiving blanket.)

Welcome the children and gather around the table. Say: **Today we're going to talk about babies. And we're going to learn about a special baby—Jesus.**

Discuss the items on the table and how they're used for babies. Then cover the items with the receiving blanket. Ask children to cover their eyes while you remove one item. Uncover the items and see if children can name the missing one. Play this game several times, but quit before children lose interest.

2. What Do You Know About Babies?

Gather in a circle, sit down and discuss:

● **How many of you have a baby in your home?**

● **How many of you have played with a baby?**

● **What do babies do?**

● **Where are babies born?**

● **What can you tell me about Jesus when he was a baby?**

● **What do we call the special day when Jesus was born?**

Say: **Babies do all kinds of things. They giggle.** (Ask kids to giggle.) **They cry.** (Ask kids to cry.) **They like to be hugged.** (Tell kids each to hug the people sitting on both sides of them.)

Jesus was a baby too. He giggled, cried and liked to be hugged. He was born long ago in a town called Bethlehem. We celebrate his birthday on Christmas.

3. Action-Packed Story

Ask children to stand. Lead them in the following action-packed Christmas story.

Jesus and Mary had to take a trip on a donkey. (Walk in place, pretend to pull a stubborn donkey.)

Joseph and Mary looked for a place to stay. (Look around, up high, down low, under things.)

The innkeeper had no room for them. (Shake head.)

Mary and Joseph slept on the stable floor. (Lie on the floor.)

When Jesus was born, they wrapped him up. (Pretend to wrap a baby and cuddle him.)

Mary laid him in a manger. (Pretend to lay baby down.)

Mary and Joseph thanked God. (Fold hands, look to heaven.)

4. Snackin' Time

(You'll need applesauce—served in baby-food jars if possible, spoons and napkins.)

Ask kids to follow you to a snack table. March to this chant:

Time, time, time to eat.
Follow me to a little treat!

Have children think about babies who eat real baby food from the jars.

5. Jesus' Birthday

(You'll need a children's Bible.)

Tell children to continue eating their snack and listen to a story about the very first Christmas. Read Luke 2:1-20. Ask:

● **What town was Jesus born in?**
● **Where did he sleep?**
● **What did he wear?**

Say: **Jesus was born in a place where they kept animals—something like a barn. His bed was a manger—what they used to hold food for animals. He wore cloths that wrapped all around him to keep him warm.**

6. Wrapping Baby Jesus

(You'll need the "Baby Jesus" handout, scrap fabric cut in strips, crayons and glue.)

Ask kids to follow you to the table with the supplies. Tell them they're going to remember that first Christmas—baby Jesus' birthday—by wrapping Jesus in swaddling clothes.

Give each child a "Baby Jesus" handout. Have them each color baby Jesus' face. Then help them each glue the fabric strips to Jesus' body.

7. Rattle Rhymes

(You'll need one baby rattle for each child. Church nurseries usually have plenty.)

Give children each a baby rattle. Read the following word groups. In each group, have the children listen for the word that relates to Jesus' birth. When they hear one, kids should shake their rattle. Do the first one or two with them.

Ball, <u>baby</u>, bubble
Bowl, bicycle, <u>Bethlehem</u>
Caterpillar, <u>Christmas</u>, cartwheel

BABY JESUS

Minnie, Mollie, <u>Mary</u>
Monkey, <u>manger</u>, Montana
<u>God</u>, golf, green

Say: **Jesus was a real baby, a lot like babies you've seen. And he is also God. He came to earth as a baby and then grew up to save us from our sins.**

8. Christmas Sing-Along

(You'll need pots, pans, lids, spoons and bowls—anything that can be used as a musical instrument.)

Show children the variety of kitchen utensils. Invite them each to create a musical instrument, make a sound or beat a rhythm and then practice. For example, hit two lids together, click two spoons together, use a spoon to tap on a bowl or pan.

Sing some of the kids' favorite Christmas songs such as "Away in a Manger" and "Joy to the World." Direct the instrumentalists to play as they sing.

9. Christmas Prayer

Ask kids to hold their instruments quietly as you pray. You'll signal them to "make a joyful noise" at the end of the prayer.

Pray: **Thanks for babies, God. Thanks especially for baby Jesus and his birthday—Christmas.**

Ask kids to play their instruments as they shout "Merry Christmas!"

by Nanette Goings

CONTRIBUTORS

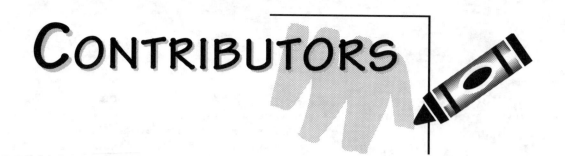

Karen M. Ball is an editor in Illinois.

Patti Chromey works with children in her church in Missouri.

Nanette Goings is the mother of two preschoolers and an art coordinator for children in a church in Colorado.

Jerayne Gray-Reneberg is a minister in Colorado and has worked with children of all ages.

Ray and Cindy Peppers live in Georgia, where he is a Christian educator and she is an insurance agent.

Jolene L. Roehlkepartain, former Editor of CHILDREN'S MINISTRY Magazine, is a freelance writer in Minnesota.

Jane P. Wilke is an early childhood educator in Missouri.

Paul Woods, former Managing Editor of Group Books & Curriculum, is an editor and freelance writer in Michigan.

Christine Yount is Editor for CHILDREN'S MINISTRY Magazine.

INNOVATIVE RESOURCES FOR CHILDREN'S MINISTRY

LIVELY BIBLE LESSONS

You can make creative teaching a snap with these 20 complete children's Bible lessons for each age level. Lively is better, because kids learn more. Each lesson has at least six child-size activities including easy-to-do crafts, action songs, attention-grabbing games, and snacks that reinforce the message. Plus, innovative new lessons are included to celebrate holidays like Valentine's Day, Easter, Thanksgiving, and Christmas. Just read the simple instructions, gather a few easy-to-find supplies, and you're ready to go!

Grades K-3
ISBN 1-55945-074-6

Kindergarten
ISBN 1-55945-097-5

Grades 1-2
ISBN 1-55945-098-3

MAKING SCRIPTURE STICK

Lisa Flinn & Barbara Younger

Discover 52 unforgettable Bible verse adventures for children in grades 1-5. You'll use creative, hands-on learning techniques that draw kids into a world of imagination, discovery, and creative interaction. Bible verses come alive with these active, fun adventures as kids...

- make paper tambourines and use them to create a new song of praise (Psalm 150:4);
- run finger races and discuss the challenges that Christians face (Hebrews 12:1);
- blow bubbles and see that bubbles last an instant while God's love is forever (Psalm 90:2); and
- make a foot-paint footprint banner and see how God watches their every step (Job 31:4).

The easy-to-prepare lessons feature a simple format, clear directions, inexpensive materials, reproducible handouts, and a wide variety of exciting activities. And follow-up discussions make the Bible messages stick!

ISBN 1–55945–093-2

Available at your local Christian bookstore. Or write:
Group Publishing, Inc., Box 485, Loveland, CO 80539.

MORE CREATIVE RESOURCES FOR CHILDREN'S MINISTRY

QUICK GAMES FOR CHILDREN'S MINISTRY

Discover 100 active, creative games for kids from preschool through sixth grade. More than just filling time, you'll use these games to...

- increase Bible knowledge,
- teach teamwork,
- reinforce your lesson,
- build group unity, and
- have fun!

Each game has been field-tested by children's workers from across the country. Plus, you'll appreciate how quick and easy these games are to prepare—with few or no supplies needed! Perfect for use in Sunday school, vacation Bible school, children's church, summer camp—wherever you have a group of kids.

ISBN 1-55945-157-2

SUNDAY SCHOOL SPECIALS

Lois Keffer

Discover 13 fun, Bible-based programs chock-full of creative ideas for classes of ages 4 to 12. You'll save time and money—just gather a few common, inexpensive items... photocopy the student handouts... and you're ready to teach creative Bible lessons your kids will love. Each lesson comes complete with...

- active-learning experiences—to catch kids' interest... and teach them lessons they'll remember,
- interactive Bible stories—to help even the youngest kids grasp the real meaning of Scripture,
- life applications—to encourage children to use what they've learned,
- take-home handouts—so children can share what they've learned with their families,

...and more, including tips for better understanding your kids. Plus, each creative program allows you to group children ages 4 to 12 in the same class! Use this option whenever...

- lots of families go on vacation—leaving just a few kids in each class,
- you want to give your teachers some time off,
- you're having a special-event Sunday,
- you just want to do something different in Sunday school,

...or any other time you need to combine children of different ages in the same class. Plus, 2 of the lessons offer you the additional option of including parents, grandparents, and other adults in the class.

ISBN 1-55945-082-7

Available at your local Christian bookstore. Or write:
Group Publishing, Inc., Box 485, Loveland, CO 80539.